"OUR DAUGHTER," SARAH SAID.

I looked down. Natasha's face was red, her eyes were closed. She was so small. I recognized her face from the ultrasound images. She had finally come out to live with us.

I hadn't thought much in advance about how this moment was going to feel. Mostly I had just hoped that everyone would survive, and I'd left it at that. But now it had happened. Natasha was alive and well. I was a father.

She was the most beautiful and amazing thing I'd ever seen. She was less than five minutes old—just like in the Stevie Wonder song—but already I loved her more than anything or anyone else in the world. I reached out for the rail on the bed to steady myself, suddenly realizing that I might pass out.

No matter what else ever happens to me, I know that this was the best moment of my life. Everything good in me, and everything worthwhile in this universe we try and fail to understand, touched me at that moment and I was forever changed.

Most of this book is about what you can do for your child. But you'll soon find out what your child will do for you. Your child will make your heart ache with love. She will make you *feel* more than you ever did before. Sometimes I think that Natasha gave me faith in myself, because she showed me how great my capacity for love is. I'll always be grateful to her for that.

Do I Look Like a Daddy to You?

A Survival Guide for First-time Fathers

Quinton Skinner

D T P
Trade Paperbacks

A DELL TRADE PAPERBACK

Published by
Dell Publishing
a division of
Random House, Inc.
1540 Broadway
New York, New York 10036

Copyright © 2001 by Quinton Skinner

BOOK DESIGN BY GLEN M. EDELSTEIN

Dell books may be purchased for business or promotional use
or for special sales. For information please write to:
Special Markets Department, Random House, Inc.,
1540 Broadway, New York, NY 10036.

DTP and the colophon are trademarks of Random House, Inc.

Library of Congress Cataloging-in-Publication Data

Skinner, Quinton, 1968–
Do I look like a daddy to you? : a survival guide for first-time fathers /
Quinton Skinner.
p.   cm.
Includes index.
ISBN 978-0-440-50914-1
1. Fatherhood.   2. Pregnancy—Popular works.   3. Infants—Care.
4. Father and infant.   I. Title.

HQ756 .S5455 2001
306.874'2—dc21
00-052376

Published simultaneously in Canada

146604632

For Natasha

CONTENTS

ACKNOWLEDGMENTS

Thanks, Ginny, for the idea.

Love and gratitude to my friends and family for graciously allowing me to depict them in this book.

Thanks to Jacob Hoye and Elizabeth Ziemska, for getting this project started; Alička Pistek, for her continued support, good advice, and belief in my work; and in particular Robin Michaelson, for her sensitive and astute contributions toward the final stages of molding the manuscript into a book.

Thanks to Carol Larson for her insights and humor, and for taking good care of Natasha while I was writing this book.

And for Sarah, a word something like *thanks,* but about a million times stronger and which doesn't fade when the sound is over.

NOTE TO THE READERS

This book contains practical advice and information relating to pregnancy, childbirth, and child care, based on the author's personal experiences as a new father. It is not intended to replace the advice of your obstetrician or pediatrician. Parents and parents-to-be should regularly consult with their physicians/pediatricians in matters relating to the health, diet, and development of children and pregnant women.

PROLOGUE
Do I Look Like a Daddy?

Did I look like a Daddy? Well, *I* didn't think so, not even after the birth of my daughter, Natasha, on December 5, 1998. When she came home from the hospital Natasha set upon a strict regimen of sleeping, eating, and soiling her diapers. She was a perfect little creature, totally dedicated to her own survival and growth.

And what about me? Well, it was wintertime in Minnesota. The phrase *cabin fever* does scant justice to the sensation of pressing one's cheek to a cold windowpane and looking out on a frozen street that had sighed with greenery and life just months before. Sarah, my wife, and I were largely housebound with newborn Natasha, and in my rare spare moments I dared a look at the mirror in the bathroom.

Dad. *Daddy.* That was me. At least that was what I was supposed to be. But the guy in the mirror looked suspiciously like my old self. Where was the confidence, the paternal gravitas that I had hoped I would assume upon the birth of my first child? Where was the man who looked like he knew what he was doing?

The winter finally relented when Natasha was about two

months old. It was still cold, the sky slate gray. But it was at least warm enough to go for a walk with Sarah and the baby—until then, we had tried to keep Natasha's newborn lungs protected from the harsh subzero temperatures. Natasha was becoming aware of her world just as the first hint of a spring thaw tinged the air.

We took Natasha to the toy store and checked out the stuffed animals. We carried her to the supermarket, to the urban lakes near our house, and for long strolls through the neighborhood. I liked to think of us as a mobile unit, rough and ready. We had survived the chaos and uncertainty of Natasha's early infancy—and instead of killing us, it had made us stronger.

The first thing I noticed was that people were looking at me differently. I had changed in the eyes of the world. I was a *Daddy,* and it was going to take some getting used to.

There were the old ladies, who all seemed to melt over the baby. There were other parents, with whom I was already sharing knowing nods and little smiles of commiseration. Young women looked on with warmth and interest, perhaps seeing in Natasha a facsimile of the offspring they dreamed of having one day.

And then there were the young men—guys my age and younger. I had just turned thirty, graduating from an extended postadolescence period of uncertainty and self-focus. I had been married since 1991—to Sarah, whom I met in college in California—but until then I had walked the earth unencumbered by children. Of course, I had checked out fathers, with fascination and sympathy. Now I saw the same look directed at me.

Some guys pretended not to notice the baby, walking past with studied nonchalance. A few brave souls dared a glance at Natasha, then turned away quickly as though she was a little Medusa (not a bad name, by the way, I suddenly realized one day).

Others simply took a good long look at me.

I could tell what they were thinking: *Good lord, he's carrying a baby.* Some exhibited an instinctive concern over seeing me trapped by unkind fate—maybe I was in need of some sort of fraternal rescue attempt. Others seemed to search my features for signs of my misery, while some seemed merely curious: *What kind of idiot would allow himself to be enslaved by a crying mess of drool and shit?* An unkind assessment of an infant, perhaps, but nonetheless a fair description of the average guy's perception.

Few young men dislike children—they simply can't imagine ever having one. We're *guys.* It doesn't matter how well educated we might be, or what our station is in life, we still have an X and a Y chromosome. For us, the prospect of fatherhood is basically on the same plane as the possibility of a giant meteor impacting the earth: it's unlikely, hopefully preventable, and ultimately too frightening to think about for long.

Well, now *I'm* a dad. I wasn't always a dad. When I used to see a father holding a baby, I thought he was either a poor sap or else an *übermensch* possessed with talents and levels of forbearance that I would never attain. Now I live on The Other Side. I'm someone's Daddy, and it's the best thing that ever happened to me.

If you're reading this book, chances are you're going to be a father soon, or else you already are one. Your life is changing in ways that would have been incomprehensible to you even a year ago. And you're pretty much winging it. That's how it works.

When Natasha was three months old, I found myself in a fairly unique situation for a new father. Because I work as a freelance writer, my days are my own to structure pretty much as I please. Sarah and I both have to work to make ends meet; as a lawyer, her work schedule is far less flexible than mine. We decided that it would be good for Natasha to meet other children and experience life outside the home in day care; at the same time, we knew how beneficial it was for a small child to be around her parents. We hit upon a compromise: Natasha would go to day care half the day, and I would take care of her the other half. I'd get time to work, and I'd also have time to spend with our daughter.

Sounds simple, right? Well, it was anything but. It was a juggling act that unfolded in new ways every single day. I had never taken care of a baby before, and I hadn't been alone much with Natasha until it was time for Sarah to return to work. I picked up some knowledge those first few months to get me started, and then I plunged right into the deep end of the pool. For about seven hours a day it was me and Natasha: *man vs. niña*.

I faced the big questions. *Why won't she sleep? Why won't she eat? Is she sick? How in the world am I going to entertain her for another six hours and forty-five minutes?*

In the big picture it all worked out. Natasha and I have forged a close relationship from all the hours we've logged together. But it wasn't easy—for me or for her. I made mistakes, I got stressed out, I felt overwhelmed. But soon she got older and the days got easier. I started to realize how much I had learned about being the father of a baby.

Fatherhood. I got there a little before you, and I picked up a thing or two along the way. Be patient with me, hear what I have to say, and feel free to disagree. With any luck I'll pass on a thing or two that might ease your passage into fatherhood. It isn't easy; sometimes it's no fun at all. But it's best, I think, to hear about the hard parts before you experience them. And take it from me—it's worth it in the end.

Most childbirth and early-parenting books focus on the process of pregnancy, dividing the conversation into the first, second, and third trimesters of pregnancy, and then the baby at birth, at three months, six months, a year. That makes sense for women, particularly during pregnancy.

But it's different for men. It's easy to joke about how men get off easy—we don't have to deal with pregnancy, weight gain, the pain of birth. And it's *true;* in a lot of ways nature has dealt us an easier hand to play.

But that's not the whole story. Our role in our partner's pregnancy is hard to define, and it's difficult to know precisely what we're supposed to be doing. When our child is born, at first she tends to be more attached to her mother. We might feel left out, adrift, improvising without a plan. So although men may get off easier than women in many respects, that doesn't mean our role is a simple matter.

Pregnancy for women is experienced, logically enough, as a linear progression from conception through birth: with each month there are reasonable, expected developments. In the meantime, men are preoccupied by several big issues: our financial viability, the loss of our freedom, how to handle our role in the birth of our child. Instead of a logical progression, our experience tends to be a sort of intellectual and emotional spiral, growing ever outward.

I try to mirror this process in this book, reflecting the major preoccupations that lie beneath the surface of your experience throughout pregnancy. After your baby's birth I tackle the more practical aspects of first-time fatherhood: how to take care of the baby, how to know when the baby is all right, and how to keep your relationship with your partner healthy and thriving under trying circumstances.

This book focuses on the experiences of new fathers—what they face, and how they can deal with it. I don't offer a comprehensive picture of pregnancy, and I don't pretend to tell you everything you're going to need to know about baby care. There are lots of books out there for those topics, written by experts in pediatrics and childhood development. You probably won't need to buy those books—look across the room at what your partner is reading and ask if you can read it when she's done.

I hope I can provide something to you that you won't find in other books—the experience of first-time fatherhood. It's almost certainly true that the circumstances of my life and yours are different. I know more than one kind of dad. I know married dads, single dads, divorced dads, gay dads, weekend dads. I know rich dads and poor dads. But all dads have this in common— they've been through the wars, and they came out loving their children. Soon you'll enter into the fraternal community of dads throughout the world. Fatherhood will grant you a broader perspective on life, the world, and ultimately yourself. You're about to be challenged, and you're going to change.

But let's not get ahead of ourselves. There's also plenty to say about diapers, sleep deprivation, and day care.

Do I Look Like
a Daddy to You?

1

The Moment of Truth

Your Transformation Into a Father-to-Be

Maybe you and your partner were planning to have a child together, maybe you weren't. Some of us are somewhere in between, ready to have a baby but simply letting nature take its course. Whatever you intended, the test has come back and the results are incontrovertible: you're going to be a Daddy.

People talk about remembering precisely where they were when they learned that President Kennedy was assassinated or that Elvis had died. When a man learns that he's going to be a father, it's a moment of such great impact that he'll remember it forever. Everything in his life changes in an instant. And it's just the beginning of a lifelong journey. It might be hard to believe now, but in a couple of years he'll be hard pressed to remember what life was like before his child came into the world.

Welcome to the club, my friend. You're going to be someone's Daddy.

$O YOU'VE RUINED YOUR LIFE

i remember where I was when they got me.

I had been married to my wife, Sarah, for more than six years. We met in California, lived in Los Angeles, then moved to the Boston area when she was accepted into law school. We had relocated to Minneapolis the year before and bought a house. Life was good. My career was going well. I quit smoking and started working out. Soon I was going to turn thirty, a milestone that I was anticipating with more optimism than dread. I felt as though I had ironed out some of my internal wrinkles in my twenties, and that I had started to develop a talent for being happy and contented—something that had eluded me in the postcollege years.

Sarah had always wanted to have children, ever since she was a little girl, and she had been clear to me about this fact from the beginning of our relationship. We had even talked baby names amidst the initial surge of hormonal fireworks between us, just before we graduated from college. I had never thought about having children, but Sarah's desire to have them was fine with me. *Anything* she wanted would have been fine with me—I fell for her the moment we met. Having children was part of the future, an aspect of the life we fantasized about living together.

Years went by. The time never seemed right to have a kid. Sarah came down with a wicked case of baby fever during law school, and to alleviate the symptoms I took her to a pet store. We bought a little gray kitten that we named Nora—after James Joyce's wife. After we moved to Minneapolis we decided that it was *time*. Sarah threw out the birth-control pills and we started *trying*.

I loved to say it to my friends: *We're trying*. It sounded ridiculous, almost burlesque. It sounded like we were involved in some sort of arduous task, when of course the reality was the opposite.

At this point, the prospect of having a child was little more real to me than, say, Nepal. I knew it was out there someplace, but I had never seen it, never lived there. Maybe someday, maybe not. It wasn't something I really thought about much. Which was probably healthy.

Nothing happened. Turns out it takes a little time for some women to become fertile again after taking the Pill. Who knew? We got tired of *trying*, and when Sarah started looking for a new job we put the baby-making plans on hold yet again. We started using spermicide as birth control. I liked this, because I got to brag that I was a *spermicidal maniac*.

I forget the brand name of the spermicide. But if the company ever calls me asking for suggestions, I'll recommend *You Asked For It Spermicide*. The advertising copy would read: *Don't Kid Yourself Thinking This Stuff Actually Works*.

In the spring I traveled to Russia on a writing project. I returned home with memories of St. Petersburg snowfalls fresh in my mind just as the Minnesota tundra started to thaw. I mulled over the desultory state of our garden, and started to look forward to softball season. There was a bloom in my mind to match the buds starting to appear on the trees.

I didn't know it at the time, of course, but the first thing I did after returning from Russia was to father my oldest child.

A couple of weeks later, Sarah came down with a perplexing illness. She was nauseous and experienced spells of vertigo. She suffers from migraines, so I worried that her condition had somehow worsened. The doctor diagnosed an inner-ear problem. That sounded right. The good old inner ear. *Case closed.*

Friday night approached. I had a standing appointment with my friend Brynnar, who was starting grad school that fall. Every Friday night we drank cocktails at his place until after midnight, listening to music and bullshitting, activities at which we both excelled.

Brynnar had just broken up with his girlfriend and moved

into an apartment of his own. The air was warm that night as I cycled over, a few LPs stuffed in my backpack. Sarah was planning to recover from the workweek with a long bath.

"Hey, man," Brynnar said as I carried my bike inside.

"Long time no see," I replied. We stared at each other for about ten seconds. Finally Brynnar cracked. "Cocktail?" he asked.

"Maybe just one."

Friday night was our opportunity to act like kids again. We played old Dylan and Replacements records. We smoked cigarettes, and they tasted heavenly since I wasn't smoking otherwise. I was sitting on a sofa we'd rescued from the Salvation Army about a month before, along with the retro-style coffee table on which my feet now rested.

"I think this place is really shaping up," Brynnar said with pride.

"It's looking damned good," I agreed. We surveyed his kingdom. His apartment was symbolic of a fresh start of his own. He had painted, fixed a few things, made the place more of a home.

"Not bad for a slacker," he observed.

"You won't be able to call yourself that much longer," I told him. "Not after you're a card-carrying grad student."

Brynnar lit another cigarette. "I don't know about that," he said. "I'll bet I can hold out a little longer."

We had a few more drinks. I started to sing along with Neil Young, a feat I can accomplish only after a few strong drinks.

"I love this apartment," I enthused with a slight slur. "And you got it all to yourself. Man. This is the life."

"Listen to you," Brynnar said, shaking his head. "*You're* the one with the super life. Great wife. That big old pad. You live like a pharaoh."

Brynnar and I always, at some point in the evening, took advantage of the opportunity to reflect on how much we appreciated the other's lifestyle. I was about to elaborate on this point when I happened to look up at the clock. It was almost twelve. I would have sworn it was only ten-thirty.

"You really do live it up," I said. "Your apartment is looking great. You can date whoever you want. You got it *going on*."

Brynnar nodded appreciatively. "Glad you see things the way I do," he said. His eyes were swimming behind his glasses like a triple-grape jackpot in a Vegas slot machine.

"But, as you observed, *I'm* the luckiest guy in the world," I added.

"Say, are you guys still trying to have kids?" Brynnar asked.

I exhaled with what I hoped was appropriate gravitas. Then I went into an uncomfortable riff about the strangeness of the term *trying*, until I saw from Brynnar's expression that I'd already run that one by him more than once. Finally I just shook my head.

"No," I said. "I think we're gonna put it off for a while."

"So you have a little more time," Brynnar said. He sounded as though he were speaking to a man whose life sentence had been commuted.

"I'll drink to that," I said.

By the time I left, it was about one-thirty, and the streets were nearly deserted.

When I got home, things started to go a little wrong. I wrestled the bike inside the front door, scraping my shins on the pedals. My cats stared at me in alarm, appalled by my display of noisome bad coordination—and at such a late hour. I poured myself a glass of water and flopped down on the living room sofa, ready for bed.

Not so fast, my friend, said an inner voice. I closed my eyes and leaned back. Funny. I didn't remember the house pitching on a stormy sea when I'd bought it. I opened my eyes, shut them again. No doubt about it: I was on the verge of getting *the spins*. Going upstairs right away and getting into bed, I knew, might turn out to be a mistake.

What the hell. I was still feeling pretty good. I dimmed the lights, cued up the new Bob Dylan CD, lay back down on the couch, and let the first verse of the first song wash over me.

The next thing I knew there was light streaming through the window. I looked around, blinking. Someone seemed to have replaced my eyes with cotton balls at some point during the night. My mouth felt like it was filled with rough-grade sandpaper. I was still fully dressed, my shoes still on my feet. I had fallen asleep on the sofa without even the luxury of a pillow under my head.

Suddenly I realized I wasn't alone. Sarah was standing at the foot of the couch. Ah-ha, that's why I was no longer sleeping. She was saying something to me. I sort of half sat, rubbing my face.

"What time is it?" I croaked.

"Six," she told me.

I nodded. Six in the morning. A fine time to get up. If you're a farmer and there are cows to be milked.

Wait a minute. Something wasn't right. It was Saturday morning. We never got up so early on the weekend.

My vision started to focus. Sarah was holding something in her hand. A plastic wand.

"What's that?" I asked.

"A pregnancy test," she replied.

"A pregnancy test," I repeated. She had a strange expression on her face. I hadn't noticed she had bought a pregnancy test; she hadn't voiced her suspicions to me until she knew for sure.

I sat up all the way. *Hold on a second.*

"It's positive," she said, looking into my eyes.

I realized I smelled terrible, like a distillery that had been set up on a mountain of old cigarette butts. The second thing I needed to do was take a shower and have some coffee. The first thing I needed to do was take her hand.

"I'm so happy," I said.

And that was the truth. I felt total, unconditional happiness. I was surprised to feel such unadulterated joy. It was going to be a few more hours before my head stopped throbbing and the real worrying began.

THE MOMENT OF CLARITY

Your spouse's pregnancy test comes back positive. Your life has changed forever. It might be a surprise, it might be something you planned. It might be the fulfillment of all your dreams, it might hit you like a freight train. At this defining moment, it doesn't really matter.

She'll need to go to a doctor, where she'll be given a more sophisticated test that will invariably yield the same result: You're in. They got you. You're going to be someone's dad.

Don't try to take it in all at once—your head will spin if you do. Up until now you've probably been like one of Odysseus' lotus-eaters—lazy, blissful, escapist. You might have a totally different image of yourself, but in the months to come you'll probably discover how sheltered and solipsistic you've been.

Now, you might ask yourself: Is this what I want? Am I ready?

Well, here's an important lesson: *It's not all about you anymore.* You're going to have to muddle through and do the best you can. To put it bluntly, your feelings are never going to be quite as important again. You're going to have new considerations.

If there's any question whether your spouse might be pregnant, it's not a good idea to adopt a wait-and-see attitude—especially if she drinks alcohol, smokes, or does anything else that might harm a fetus. Nature has built-in a grace period between the moment of conception and the time at which the fetus begins to ingest everything the mother does—about two weeks; basically, long enough to figure out what's happening and take action. You can get a home pregnancy test over the counter at any drugstore. If it comes up positive, the mother-to-be needs to see a doctor and make sure she understands the diet and lifestyle regimen she needs to follow to ensure a healthy baby. It's human nature not to want to learn about news that might be hard to handle, but facts are facts. If she's pregnant, she'll feel much better in the long run knowing she did everything the right way.

Hopefully the prospect of becoming a father makes you happy and fills you with optimistic thoughts of the future. It's also possible that you're full of anxiety and misgivings. For just about every father-to-be, the reality is a combination of the two. It's going to shift from moment to moment. Few of us can come to terms with big changes right away. Don't be too hard on yourself if you have a rough time.

Focus on the positive. Whatever your situation, however much money you have or don't have, no matter what the future springs on you, you're going to be a father until the end. Your child is going to admire you, and love you unconditionally. No matter how good or bad your own childhood might have been, soon you'll have a chance to contribute something good to the world—a whole new person, raised with love and caring, with as good a chance as any of us of living a good life. It's probably going to be the most noble and worthy thing you ever do.

But what about money? What about the apartment you live in, the one that barely has enough room for the two of you? What about the quality of your relationship with the mother of your child, and your prospects for the future? And what about your dreams, what about all the things you hoped to accomplish before becoming a father? And what about this crummy world of ours—what does it mean to bring a new life into it?

Calm down. Take a deep breath. Every father worries about these things, and for good reason—it's *reality*, and you're going to confront it in new ways. *Your* father worried about the very same things. Don't try to absorb the big picture all at once. And remember: you have nine months to get your head together.

"YOU'RE WHAT?"

For some couples, pregnancy is the result of careful planning. The mother's ovulation cycles are plotted against the spinning of the heavens, and everything works out fine. Some couples have experienced fertility problems, and learning of the conception of their child is a long-awaited moment. When the news comes, it's a relief and a cause for joy. *It worked. We're finally getting what we wanted.*

For others, it's a total surprise. You might be in a committed relationship, and might not. Maybe you're living together, maybe you each have your own place. Maybe, like me, you were with the same woman for a long time, completely committed, but you hadn't been explicitly trying to conceive at that particular moment. The combinations and varieties are endless.

And maybe, in your heart of hearts, you know you're not even close to being ready to become someone's father.

OK. This is probably as good a place as any to enter into a reasoned, balanced debate about the option of abortion. I'll discuss the various viewpoints and philosophies. . . .

Yeah, right. And then I'll stick a needle in my eye just to see how it feels.

If you're reading this book, you're going to be a father. Whatever your living situation, your relationship status, your religious beliefs or political ideology, you've gotten someone pregnant and you want to do the right thing. You've been dealt a hand at the table. You're *in the game.*

At this point you need to clarify your primary goal. Your number one goal, the objective from which all other actions should spring, is to be a good father. Whisper it to yourself: *I am going to be a good father.* It has a nice sound to it, doesn't it?

How you handle the initial news of your spouse's pregnancy is very important. When she tells you she's going to have your child, she's coming to you with the most important news of her life. This is probably what she's been waiting for, what she's fantasized about since she was a little girl. The news, for her, is also bringing up all kinds of thoughts. She's dealing with doubts about her self-worth, her security in your relationship, her hopes for and fears about the future.

Don't mess this up. This is not the time to focus on your trepidation, or to talk about how you had really hoped to wait a few more years. This is not the time for a prolonged examination of *your* feelings. This is not the time to talk about how *your* father made you call him "sir," and how he stormed onto the field during Little League to take you out of the game after you dropped a fly ball.

And this is *really, really* not the time to ask whether it's yours.

This is your moment to take her in your arms and tell her that this is the most wonderful news you've ever heard. This is the time to talk about the future, and about the great life you're going to provide for your child. Tell her she's going to be a great mother, and that you couldn't be happier to be having a baby with her.

You're only going to get one good chance at this. *Don't blow it.* If you've been a self-absorbed jerk up until now, fix things. This is one of the great undertakings of your life, and you don't want it to start off on the wrong foot.

Put down this book; go find the mother of your child. Tell her how great you feel, and how wonderful she is. Then come back. There's a lot more to talk about.

Once you've verified that your partner is pregnant, you'll want to give some thought to whom you tell about it. One cause for caution is the risk of miscarriage, which declines throughout the first trimester. A miscarriage can be very emotionally difficult, and the hurt can be compounded by having to relate the news to everyone whom you informed about the pregnancy. Some couples share the news with only close relatives and friends until they feel confident that the fetus is healthy and viable.

You might feel tempted to use the phrase "We're pregnant." I hear it all the time, and it never fails to puzzle me. *How can a guy get pregnant? Seems to me there's only one pregnant person involved.* This figure of speech smacks of a guy taking credit for some heavy lifting he isn't going to be doing in crunch time. "We're pregnant," of course, tries to acknowledge the fact that the pregnancy period requires a partnership, but it always sounds a bit cloying to these ears.

BEING A MAN ABOUT IT

For the past several years I'd been trying on for size the concept of being a man. *Being an adult.* I was in a very happy marriage. I had bought a house, spending dozens of hours in the bank's mortgage office sweating through the minutiae of my financial life. I felt pretty grown-up most of the time, though there was a nagging sense somewhere deep inside me that I still carried a strong residue of my boyhood and college self. My inner voice was one part adult and one part panicked adolescent. In short, I was like pretty much everyone else.

For me, irrevocable adulthood was always a step or two ahead in the hazy mists of the future. I was climbing the hill, but

I was a long way from reaching the point at which I could survey the landscape with Olympian dispassion.

Learning that I was going to be a father pushed my doubts about adulthood into the background. At once the vague outlines of the distant future were turning pretty damned distinct. I realized how many times I had set up fatherhood as a sort of arbitrary deadline. *When I'm a father, I'll stop smoking. I'll start taking better care of myself. I'll really get motivated about my career. I'll deal with my anger, my self-centeredness, and all of those parts of myself that I'm ashamed of.*

Well, it didn't exactly work out that way. Learning I was going to become a father didn't turn me instantly into a new person. I had already quit smoking, but I started otherwise taking better care of myself. I tried to think more about my financial future, and I got more serious about trying to improve my character.

Fatherhood gradually came into focus, like nearly every change in life does; after the initial shock came gradual adjustment. The sun rose in the morning and I was still me—for better and worse. The fetus inside my wife grew every day, but on the outside things were pretty much the same.

Hmm, I thought. This seemed like a problem. Things were the same. Wasn't everything going to change? Wasn't something *more* supposed to be going on?

Pretty soon I realized that something was going on after all. I lay in bed one night, staring at the ceiling, thinking about my next freelance job and the fact that I didn't know who I would be working for next year. I worried about nuclear war, and diseases. I worried about dying in a car accident before my child was old enough to take care of herself. I worried about the collapse of society, about the cruelties of life. I worried over just about everything. I thought the foundation of my house might be crumbling, and about the possibility that someday I might not be able to pay my mortgage. I worried about my health, I worried about Sarah.

After about an hour of this I got out of bed. I went downstairs and turned on the lights. I poured a glass of wine and sat down at the dining room table. All was quiet. The cats circled me cautiously, sensing that I needed to be alone with my thoughts.

The future was so big, so vast, so beyond my control. I was starting to understand what an effort it was going to take to keep control of my insignificant little part of the universe. I knew that I was going to make mistakes, plenty of them, and that I wouldn't even recognize some of my errors until long after the damage was done. I thought about my child, so young that she wasn't even recognizable as a human. She lived inside my wife, growing slowly, not even thinking yet.

I finished my glass of wine, rinsed it, put it in the cupboard. I turned off the lights and walked back up the creaky stairs. It was after one, and I got back in bed gently, careful not to wake Sarah. After about a half hour, I drifted off.

I didn't realize it at the time, but the ritual I had just enacted had been gone through countless times by men from the beginning of our lives on this planet. I was a worried father, small and weak. It was going to take all the strength and will I possessed to take care of and protect my family.

I had taken my place in the mainspring of life, in the procession of generations from parents to children that moves through life. I may have thought I was a man before, but I wasn't.

Not until then.

THE END OF YOUR LIFE

There's a flashback sequence in an episode of *The Simpsons* in which Marge and Homer go to Dr. Hibbert and learn that Marge is pregnant. He chuckles and hands them a pamphlet. It's entitled "So You've Ruined Your Life."

So. You've ruined your life. There's nothing left in your once-bright future but dirty diapers, strollers, piano recitals, and a long, gradual descent into becoming your parents.

If you think this is what's going to happen, then you're setting yourself up for a self-fulfilling prophecy. What you're really fearing is the loss of your youthful identity and a subsuming of your goals and aspirations into the greater reality of being part of a family. You might be scared to death of turning into a sweater-wearing, pipe-smoking *dad,* someone the kids goof on when his back is turned.

First of all, children *always* laugh at their parents when their backs are turned. When it happens—and it will—consider it a hard-won badge of honor. The little shits don't know anything, anyway. They don't know the value of a dollar and they don't know the half of it. Their music is nothing but horrible noise. They wouldn't know hard work if it came up and . . .

Anyway, it's *good* that you're having these fears at this point. It means that you still have some fight in you. You're not quite ready yet to pack it in and become one of the Parenthood Zombies, the males of the species roaming the countryside and stunning their unwitting prey with long digressions on diaper services and the virtues of education-based day care.

You're still you. It's nice to keep that in mind. You're still allowed to laugh, play, have a good time. Your thoughts are still your own. Your dreams are still permitted.

But now there's a new framework for it all. Because you're going to be a father.

I realized this later the same day Sarah told me she was pregnant. We went to the movies and saw *Primary Colors,* the thinly veiled account of the Clinton campaign for the presidency. It was somehow comforting to see Bill's foibles portrayed on the giant screen. The movie allowed me to say to myself *Well, at least I'm not that screwed up.*

But when we left the theater, a new thought settled in. Going to the movies, stopping for dinner afterward—these things were going to be a lot harder to do in nine months. Our lives would no longer be our own. Every move we made would have to be considered and planned out in advance. *Good-bye, spontaneity.*

It was an immensely depressing notion at first. But I adjusted to it before too long. *Of course* nothing was ever going to be the same again. But there was no stopping. The only thing I *could* control was how I was going to deal with it.

Did I want to wallow in lamentation, bemoaning my lost youth and the changes in my life? Did I choose to feel overwhelmed by the responsibility and seemingly overpowering weight of what was to come? In other words, did I want to transform what could be the best thing in my life into a pile of crap in my mind?

Or did I want to get my attitude together and be positive?

This is the choice that faces every new father. And the answer is obvious. You *have* ruined your life—but you've ruined only the life you would have led without your child. In the bargain, you have improved your life in ways that you won't really be able to understand until you're on the other side.

CONSIDERING MARRIAGE

If you're already married, skip this section. You've made your decision already, and having a child—whether you planned to do so or not—is the natural next step.

If you're not married, you probably have some thinking to do.

My friend Kevan is a brilliant young scientist who lives in the Boston area. We met years ago in a karate class, and bonded over our shared gradual disillusionment with the system of katas and martial-arts ritual, which didn't seem to be leading anywhere. Soon we were meeting every Tuesday night at Paddy's bar in Cambridge for Irish whiskey and billiards. We stayed in touch after Sarah and I moved to Minneapolis.

By the time I learned that I was going to be a father, Kevan's daughter was about a year old already. He seemed extremely happy and very sure of himself. I always knew he had a lot of energy and optimism—these were the traits I most admired in him—but I was doubly impressed by the way he seemed to be taking fatherhood in stride.

Cathy, Kevan's partner, got pregnant for the second time when Natasha was still a baby. Around this time I remembered an obvious fact—Kevan and Cathy had never gotten married. They eventually had two children, they bought a house together, yet they hadn't decided to take the vows. I mentioned this during a phone call.

"No, we're still not married," he said.

"No kidding." I pondered for a moment. "Well, are you going to get married?"

"Nope. No plans of the sort," Kevan replied, cool as ever.

"Gotcha."

And that was that. Women sometimes find it hard to understand that this is generally the way men communicate with each other—especially about sensitive emotional issues. Kevan answered my question, and that topic of discussion was effectively concluded. I didn't really need to know his thoughts or feelings on the matter. He wasn't married, but he was living with Cathy and they had two children together. It was fine with them, it was fine with me.

If only it was that simple for everyone. There is societal pressure for a couple to get married when they're going to have a child together. Some of these pressures make sense, others are holdovers from days gone by. It wasn't so long ago that birth certificates for the offspring of unmarried couples in effect identified the children as bastards.

Today things are a bit different. Many people don't feel the need to get married: they're committed to each other through deeds rather than ceremony. I can appreciate this line of thinking. One drawback is that you'll find yourself explaining yourself to your children as you move through life, but if you're so unorthodox you probably won't mind.

There are a bevy of legal benefits to marriage that are worth bearing in mind, including assumption of paternity, visitation in hospitals, and custody in the case of death. Financial considerations such as insurance also come into play. If you have better health coverage than your partner does, you might want to get married in order to carry her—and your child—on that coverage. On the other hand, if she's happy with her insurance, and doesn't want to make a change, you might want to hold off on marriage for a while.

As far as societal pressure goes—well, if you worry about that sort of thing, you'll find no shortage of issues to fret over in every area of life. I'm not suggesting it's intrinsically bad to be concerned about the codes and norms of the world. Your families would probably be a lot happier if you and your partner were married. There's knowledge and insight into human nature behind societal traditions. It's always good to be aware, though, that we have choices.

As for getting married because your partner is pregnant—well, you wouldn't be the first. Not long after Sarah and I announced we were getting married, we were riding in the car with her father. Jeff, soon to be my father-in-law, asked in a lighthearted and offhand manner: *So, are you pregnant?* Sarah responded with an appropriately embarrassed and outraged *Dad!* but it seemed like a reasonable question to me at the time.

The real question is whether or not your partner wants to get married, and not so much what *you* want to do. You're having a child; a lot of things are going to change. Can you say for sure that she doesn't want to take a trip down the aisle, or at least to City Hall? Maybe there's a deep and profound part of her heart that craves the validation that marriage grants. Maybe she wants a husband to go along with her child. It's a reasonable desire, if you look at it from her point of view.

If you haven't already, it's time now to find out how she *really* feels. Maybe she's gone along with your iconoclastic repudiation of marriage because you've been an overbearing doctrinaire. Just a thought. You never know.

Some people claim that all marriage is is a piece of paper. Well, *sure*. A birth certificate is also just a piece of paper. But it symbolizes much more. Every couple needs to sort out their level of commitment to each other before having a child. Remember, you're going to have a lot to deal with after your child is born. You'll be best served to try to figure this one out ahead of time.

And I hear some of those maternity wedding gowns are pretty hot.

2

Your Built-in Grace Period

Pregnancy: How to Shine While Adjusting to Losing Your Freedom

OK, my friend. The initial shock has worn off.

Now your partner has been pregnant for a month or so. She's exhausted all the time, going to bed before nine and leaving you alone with your swirling thoughts. She might be nauseous, irritable, a little overwhelmed. But now you're both getting used to the idea of what's to come. The fact is, in a sense you're a father already. You'll soon be out of the statistical miscarriage-risk period, and things are hopefully going well.

So why are you sitting around with your mind swimming? Because it's perfectly *rational*. While your partner is dealing with the manifestations of your pregnancy, you're starting to realize how much your life is going to change. You're wondering what it's all going to mean. Most of all you're terrified by how much freedom you're going to lose when the baby's born.

Well, here's a little secret: you're *right* to worry. Having children cuts into your personal freedom like nothing else. But you'll adjust, and your life will be better than before if you approach it the right way. Trust me on this one.

Your focus for now should be on what you can do to help. It's time for you to start shining. Just be sure to take it as it comes, and don't try to become a perfect father all at once. There's plenty of time left for you to come to terms with your new role in life as someone's Daddy.

PREGNANCY—NATURE'S BUILT-IN GRACE PERIOD

Fortunately, humans take roughly nine months to gestate and give birth to their offspring. You could have been born a mouse, in which case you'd have about three weeks to get your mouse head together before your progeny appeared in the world. The kangaroo father has about forty days, the wolf little more than two months. (Of course, we could envy the sea lion, whose partner takes about eleven months to bear children. But I'm sure human women are quite happy that their pregnancies don't last any longer than they already do.)

Somehow, nine months will seem about right. You will have time to line your nest, put your affairs in order, and get your frame of mind as solid as it needs to be.

For my part, I got through the early days of Sarah's pregnancy by pretending that nothing out of the ordinary was going on. This is known as the *ostrich method,* and the deep sands of denial, for me, were welcoming indeed. But eventually we all have to come up for air and face the fact: fatherhood is impending.

Buy a camera if you don't already have one. Start taking pictures of your partner in her underwear. No, not *those* kinds of pictures—that's none of my business—I'm talking about taking photographs of her from the side, in front of a featureless wall. Take a new picture on the first of each month—same location, same pose. Eventually you'll have a nice little collection of smiling pregnant-belly pictures. You can pull them out when you're both eight months into the process, then look at the five-month belly and share a laugh. *We thought that was big? That was nothing. This belly here, now that's big.*

SWIMMING IN THE DEEP WATER

S arah's pregnancy, for me, was a strange mix of looming anxiety and a gnawing impatience. The baby was coming. There was an estimated time of arrival: December 1, 1998. A lot of good that did me in August. Frequently I wished the baby was born already so that I could get on with the business of being a father. But just as often, I was acutely aware that I should savor my old life as long as it lasted.

For some reason I couldn't quite explain, I didn't really like to touch Sarah's pregnant belly. Everyone else couldn't wait to get their hands on it, but not me. I worried about the baby; I imagined it was terribly fragile. I thought about everything that could go wrong. I had a superstitious fear that if I rubbed the belly, if I got too close to the magic, I would be punished with some terrible event.

I didn't know anything about pregnant women. I imagined they lay around a lot, fanning themselves with newspapers and gasping for another glass of lemonade. I guessed there were bouts of tears, followed by irrational anger—pretty much the kind of substantial information one can glean from a lifetime spent watching TV sitcoms.

I figured there was no way a woman could carry around all that extra weight for nine months. Something *had* to give. And sometimes it does: some women suffer complications that land them in bed for weeks. But that's pretty unusual. For the most part, women live normal lives during pregnancy, often right up to the point at which they go into labor.

That doesn't mean it's a picnic for them. Before you try to sort out your thoughts, make sure your partner is taken care of. Your child's mother needs your help making her life easier, especially as the pregnancy progresses. By the time your baby is born, your good habits should be completely ingrained and you'll be somewhat accustomed to the scope of your new responsibilities.

1. **Pick up the slack** on cooking and housework. Pregnant women are tired all the time, first from all the biological changes they have to endure, then from the hard work of carrying a baby in their belly. You should have *already* been doing your share of the household workload. But let's face it. We're men. It's not easy for us. We're selfish by nature, and many of us were coddled by our families and protected from the rigors of the domestic arts.

A little goes a long way. If you can't cook, open up a basic cookbook. Making a meal is a matter of following instructions. Take over the lion's share of the grocery shopping. Assume responsibility for some of those little errands your partner usually runs—the ones that benefit both of you, and which you almost never thank her for. Clean the kitchen and the bathroom more often—these jobs require bending and stretching, which is soon going to be almost impossible for her. Taking on more of the domestic burden is only right. And, believe me, she'll appreciate it.

2. **Get involved** in the pregnancy. Listen to how she's feeling and try to make her comfortable. If she's hungry, make her a snack. Ask her what kinds of vitamins she's taking and make sure she has a steady supply. Don't zone out when she wants to talk about an article she just read about the pros and cons of vaccinations. This goes against the essential nature of most men. When Sarah tells me a story about one of her coworker's children, it takes all my pow-

ers of concentration not to start thinking about Bruce Willis movies I've seen, or to wonder if it's really true that Bill Parcells has permanently retired from NFL coaching. But nature is not necessarily destiny, and we can take steps to better ourselves. A lot of what your partner says during her pregnancy, beneath the surface, is all about her concerns and hopes for your child.

Many women experience what's known as the *nesting instinct* when they're pregnant. They become energetically preoccupied with the home: making sure everything is just right, fussing over the baby's future living space. It may be totally unscientific, but it seems like there's something biological going on when a pregnant woman starts to turn the bedroom into a warm, soft, comfortable refuge from the world outside.

A lot of men experience the same thing, although it takes a different form—often involving the use of power tools and an outrageous overreaching of their home-improvement skills. Some would say to exercise caution. I say: *Go for it.* After the baby is born, you'll be too tired and preoccupied for months to do much home improvement. So go ahead. Put up those shelves. Redo that bathroom tile. Build a three-car garage that takes up all the green space in your yard. When your kid is about a year old, you'll be able to go back and repair all your mistakes.

3. Remain aware that she's going to be a parent for the first time, too, and that her life is also going to permanently change. Encourage her to take time for herself, and to get away from the house if she's feeling claustrophobic. Go out and do the shopping, leaving her in peace for a nap or to read. Pregnant women get aches and pains—you would, too, if you had a baby growing inside you. Buy her some bath salts, a new pillow; surprise her with flowers, maybe some scented aromatherapy oil. Small gestures mean a lot.

• • •

All of this boils down to putting yourself in her shoes. Try to be thoughtful, and do things without being asked. Don't worry about being a perfect spouse. Just try to be a good one.

WELCOME TO THE SIDELINES

3 eing pregnant isn't easy. And it's important to keep in mind that your partner's body starts undergoing big changes immediately after conception. The growing fetus requires huge amounts of its mother's bodily resources in order to grow, and the results are predictable: For the first trimester, the mother-to-be is tired, sometimes sick. Being pregnant plays havoc with a woman's hormones, and the result can be mood swings and irritability. As the pregnancy progresses, new problems are thrown into the mix: muscle and ligament pain, reduced mobility, and the sight of your hollow-eyed shock.

Your job for the time being is, essentially, to be as supportive as possible. Biology has placed you on the sidelines for now, but you need to be as sympathetic as possible to your partner's plight. The experience of carrying a child to term runs the gamut from transcendent bliss to extreme fatigue and frustration. It's an emotional time. It's exhausting and exhilarating. Most of all, it's *intense.*

If you want to see an illustration of what lurks in the male subconscious on the subject of pregnancy, watch the part of the movie *Alien* in which the snarling baby monster gnaws its way out of the unfortunate space traveler's chest. The baby, for now, is unseen, unknown. It's a powerful presence in both your lives. I had a dream early on in Sarah's pregnancy in which she gave birth to our calico cat Lucy. It was pretty realistic, right down to the gowned and masked doctor presenting to us our furry, wide-eyed new feline daughter.

These nine months afford you time to process the changes that are coming in your life. A man's mind can deal with only so much at any given time, and you're going to find yourself enduring a lot of psychological ups and downs. It's probably impossible for a man to truly and deeply empathize with the experience of carrying a child, and it's not in our nature to come to terms with fatherhood overnight. Don't beat up on yourself for feeling adrift and worried, or because you don't feel as *much* as you want to. Remember your limitations and cut yourself as much slack as possible.

Don't worry about the range of what you're feeling about being a father. No matter what might be going on inside your head, you're almost certainly not the first man who has ever felt this way. Whatever emotions you experience—positive and negative—you're having them *for a reason*. And that reason is to fully experience the realities of becoming a father.

I'll share something with you now, at this early stage: it's going to be great; it's going to be awful; it's going to be everything in between. Anyone who says living with a baby is always great is either lying to you or is an inveterate optimist. And anyone who says that living with a baby is a joyless hardship is a fool who's missing out on what should be the greatest thing in his life.

There are surely some men who feel totally positive about having children. The process of pregnancy, for them, must be a blissful time of uncomplicated anticipation. If this sounds like you, then great: you're going into fatherhood with a terrific attitude.

But pregnancy, for most men, is pretty scary. First of all, you'll worry that something is going to go wrong. I can tell you that this fear isn't going to vanish until the baby is born. After that, you're going to worry all the time about the happiness, safety, and well-being of your child. This is natural. This is what *paternal* feelings are all about. The important thing is not to let your worries get out of control and consume your every waking moment.

If you're having anxiety problems now that the pregnancy is progressing, don't be too proud to do something about it. For a lot of men, admitting that they're worried is like an admission of failure. But really, you'd be crazy *not* to worry. Try to exercise and eat right, and get enough sleep. If you're feeling uptight all the time, try deep-breathing techniques: Take ten deep, long breaths, in through the nose and out through the mouth. Count slowly to ten, breathe deep into your diaphragm, and don't exhale too quickly. Doesn't that feel better?

There are other measures to take. Meditation classes are available at churches and community centers. You can buy relaxation tapes that guide you through a program of unwinding and letting go. If you're really having a hard time, you might consider seeing a mental-health professional and talking through your anxieties. The more relaxed you are, the happier you'll be. And you'll become a better father.

The chances are very good that everything is going to be all right. But it's also in the realm of possibility that something could go wrong. The best thing you can do is to *stay involved*. If you're not able to go along with your partner to her checkups, debrief her afterward. Ask for details; she'll be happy to share them with you. Concrete information will go a long way toward easing your mind. Remember that pregnancy and childbirth have come a long way since even we were born. I found our health-care professionals—our midwife, doctor, and nurses—to be dedicated, knowledgeable, and sincere. After all, everyone wants the birth of a child to go well.

But there's another category of fear, one that particularly plagues expectant fathers: loss of freedom.

It isn't an easy concept to get used to.

THE END OF THE WORLD AS YOU KNOW IT

3 ecoming a father is likely to be the most dramatic change you've ever experienced. A friend of mine, a mother who lives in New York, captured the issue succinctly:

"For men, the main thing about becoming fathers is the loss of their freedom and independence," she told me. "They're afraid that their life is going to change, and they're going to lose all the things upon which they've based their identity."

I don't have much to add to that. At some point early in your partner's pregnancy—around the time you're spending your money on furniture and baby clothes instead of new CDs and weekend excursions—this will become pretty apparent.

What's going on here? you will ask yourself. *It's begun, hasn't it? The end of my life.*

Well, there's no sugarcoating it. Let's be frank. You're right. Your life *is* over.

Forgive my heavy-handed attempt at shock therapy, but every new father has to process this information in the best way he can—and better sooner than later.

Your life is over. That is, the life you have lived without children. Your familiar ways of doing things are, to a great extent, going to fade into memory. Becoming a father means that your role in the world, your concerns and preoccupations, and the ways in which you spend your energy are going to forever change. *If* you plan on doing it right.

OK, we got that out of the way. But this doesn't mean that you have to necessarily become something you don't want to be. What it does mean is that you're going to have to expand both your identity in the world and the way you view yourself. You're going to have to rummage through your habits and all the ways you deal with life; you'll discard the ones that no longer do you any good, strengthen the ones that do, and invent some new ones in order to cope.

This doesn't have to be a conscious process; change rarely is. It's going to happen whether you want it to or not, and the healthiest way to look at it is with optimism and good humor.

It's been fun being the baby of the family. If you're like most men, you've gotten to play the role well into adulthood—but now it's over.

Here's the thing about change—it always happens, and we nearly always resist it. *I like the way I am,* an inner voice keeps saying. The best answer for this is *Fine, but now you have a new identity to learn, a new role to play. Try to keep liking yourself as you adapt.*

One of the most important aspects of adjusting to fatherhood is learning not to fight the battles that don't matter—both with the outside world and within your own mind. The latter is particularly pernicious. We can spend more energy worrying about what we *don't* want to become than about what we *do* want to become.

Fatherhood is going to teach you things about yourself. All kinds of thoughts and prejudices are going to pop into your mind. *You know, guys pushing strollers look ridiculous. People who dress boys in blue and girls in pink are just playing into tired old stereotypes. I hate it when people bring their babies to parties. What's up with people with kids whose houses are strewn with toys and baby crap—I mean, don't they have any pride? Look at them in their minivans! And baby talk—that's fine in the privacy of people's homes, but do they have to inflict it on me in public? Goo goo ga ga—it makes me want to vomit.*

You might find yourself getting irritated by all kinds of things about other parents and their children. It all comes down to one guiding principle: *I'm not going to be like them.* I used to listen to parents cajoling and bargaining with their children and think, *Not me, no sir. No way am I ever going to sound like that.* And I had, and still have to a large extent, a big hang-up about people buying expensive children's clothes. It seems like a waste to me.

These are the kinds of things we can get hung up on. We become afraid of turning into something we don't want to be. Then we start to worry that becoming a father is going to change us for the worse.

But these are just distractions, junk thrown up by our minds during a difficult time. The thing about strollers—come on, strollers are *good*. They enable fathers to be more mobile. And the pink and blue thing? Well, when Gramma gives your daughter a pink dress with a big bow on it, you'd damn well better dress the kid in it and snap a picture. It's only respectful—and, believe me, it won't make you a perpetrator of gender stereotypes. *That* happens when you don't help out in the kitchen.

And the big mess of garish neon plastic and toys littering the floor of the house? *Get used to it.* If it makes you feel better, pick up the place every night after the baby goes to bed. Put the toys away in the closet and get them out the next morning. And as for spending too much money on baby clothes, I simply don't do it. But when someone gives Natasha a dress or a shirt that I wouldn't have bought out of principle, I express my genuine thanks and make sure she wears it as often as possible.

Our generation is preoccupied with identity, with being who we want to be, and much of the time this expression comes down to exterior traits and qualities as stand-ins for our inner ideals. It's a form of guilt by association. We don't want to do something because *that kind of person* does it. People coming of age in our time have become hypersensitive to image. There's nothing necessarily wrong with this. We all do it. It's who we are; it's how we live.

But as a father, you're going to be dealing with *a lot* of factors that are beyond your control. It won't be as simple as driving the right kind of car, or not driving the wrong kind. Defining your identity is going to be more nuanced than all the old ways: how we dressed, what kind of music we listened to, what kind of movies we liked.

And here's the deep secret: We were able to get away with

being so discriminating, so self-conscious, because it was *easy*. It was a game for *kids*. It made us feel good; it helped us understand who we were. But it's not going to work so easily anymore.

Having a child will be the new game in town. Your new identity is that of a father. It doesn't mean you throw away everything you were before, but you will need to shake it up and fit it in a new box.

Here's something to try on for size:

YOU WILL NOT HAVE TO BECOME A LUMPY, STYLE-LESS ZOMBIE WHEN YOU BECOME A FATHER. YOU WON'T BE REQUIRED TO BECOME EVERYTHING YOU OPPOSED IN YOUR YOUTH.

BUT YOU ALSO WON'T NEED TO WORRY ABOUT IT SO DAMNED MUCH. YOU'LL HAVE OTHER CONCERNS.

Our generation is expert at self-definition and self-expression. But it becomes a trap when we're afraid to step out of our shells and assume new roles in life. For some reason we tend to think that we had it all together in our early twenties, and that any deviation from this perfection is tantamount to failure.

It ain't so.

Change is only painful when you resist it too much. The Buddha said something along the same lines. And the best way to let it happen is not to think about yourself all the time. You can think, for instance, about your partner and your child. Then everything will fall into place.

Who *are* you going to be as a father? When Natasha was born, I struggled to get a sense of myself as her father—that looming silhouette of authority and power that hangs over every child's life, part archetype, part beloved protector, part legendary monster.

I figured I'd be all right, on the whole. I was a pretty nice guy. People seemed to like me. So I was a little irascible at times, maybe a bit proud. I could live with that. But could my child? I mean, she would only know me as a giant, an authority figure whom she would first rely upon, then inevitably rebel against.

I tried to view myself from the outside, to project an impression of myself as seen through the eyes of a small child. In my mind's eye a picture began to form of a hulking figure. His face was firm, impassive, mysterious. Who *was* it that I was seeing?

That's when it hit me. The picture I envisioned was a striking cross between Joseph Stalin and the Creature From the Black Lagoon. *Without* the ripping sense of humor that both were so well known for.

Have you met my dad? my children would ask their friends. I would grunt and lurch toward them, and the friends would run off in fright. There was *so* much to look forward to.

A GHOST OF THE MAN I KNEW

Sarah and I are friends with an English couple, Ross and Ann, who lived in the United States for a year because of Ross's job. Ross and Ann were smart, funny, and liked to make frequent casual reference to their bodily functions. It was a perfect match.

Unfortunately, their stay here came to an end when Ross was reassigned to Australia. It was an extremely depressing time—how often do you and your partner meet another couple in which all four parties get along equally well, without reservation? We saw them off one morning and sat around moping for an entire weekend.

Before they left, Ann got pregnant. There were congratulations all around, and I really enjoyed Ross's queasy expression when they broke the news to us. He was in for it, I thought. Of course, nature took vengeance on me soon enough for my *schadenfreude*—but that's another story.

We stayed in close contact with Ross and Ann through E-mail and Sunday-afternoon phone calls. A few months after they arrived in Melbourne, their daughter Meg was born. By then Sarah was pregnant, and our shared experience solidified our friendship when geographical distance could have strained it.

I started to notice something strange about Ross when I talked to him on the phone. It was the verbal equivalent of the thousand-yard stare war veterans are supposed to get after months of brutal combat.

"How are you?" Ross would ask in a weak voice.

"Great. We went to a movie today, and later on I'm going over to Brynnar's house for cocktails—after I work out at the gym. What about you?"

There was a low muttering on the line. At first I thought it was static; then I realized it was Ross.

"What's that?" I asked. "Did you say something?"

"We went for a walk today."

"That's great, that's really great," I replied. A walk? Why was he telling me this?

"Meg shit all over her clothes, though," Ross continued, his voice flat. "Had to throw away the pack I was carrying her in. There was just too much of it, man."

"Wow," I marveled.

"We might watch a video later," he added without much enthusiasm. "If we can stay up and if Meg lets us."

"What about your music?" I asked.

"No time."

"Have you been painting?" Two of Ross's macabre, funny paintings hung in my house.

"No, no place to paint," Ross said. "The baby. You know."

"Oh," I replied.

Ross didn't sound depressed. Instead he sounded as though the life had been wrung out of him—and it had, metaphorically, by a pair of tiny hands.

"Well, things will get better," I said.

He didn't reply to my empty reassurances. Instead, he asked, "When is Sarah due again? In a few more months?"

A cold chill ran up my spine. I was next.

MY DAD

When I was a little boy my dad used to take me for long walks. We'd walk for an hour or two through the city, talking about a topic of his choosing. One night it was religion, another night sex. He told me how stereos worked, and about the effects and pitfalls of drugs. I walked with my hands in my pockets and my head down, asking questions and wishing it would never end.

My parents were young when they had me, just out of high school. They were just kids, really, and they split and divorced while I was still a small child. I lived with my mother, who was the person who took care of me every day and was the center of my emotional universe. I saw my dad one night during the week, and for a sleepover on Friday or Saturday night. I never thought there was anything unusual about this arrangement, because it was all I ever knew.

Everybody's family is different. But what's the same for all of us is how becoming a father makes us think about our own childhood and our parents. We begin to understand them in ways that were never before possible. And we begin to have more sympathy for their faults and failings—those sins that might have seemed unforgivable when we were sixteen.

My dad was a strong presence in my life for as long as I can remember. He taught me a sense of responsibility, along with a nagging perfectionism. He introduced me to books and sports, two diversions that have become adult pastimes. He always challenged me, and gave me a sense that there were standards that I had to meet.

Now that I have Natasha I've begun to understand how much a child changes and defines your world. I know how much effort goes into little parental actions that are never recognized, never rewarded. I can't imagine how my mother took care of me on her own, and I know how much love she must have felt for me in order to make it through. And I realized now how difficult it must have been for my dad to see me only twice a week, to try to remain a strong force in my life without being part of my day-to-day reality.

I have a great relationship with my dad. We talk on the phone a few times a week, and stay connected on the big concerns of our lives. And I understand a little bit more today about who he is, and what his life has been.

Our children give us so much in return for our effort and affection. They teach us about love, and they hold up a mirror to our selves. They teach us about who our parents were, and who they are.

Sometimes when I'm talking to Natasha I hear my father's voice coming out of my mouth. It's a comforting sound.

3

"I'm Ruined!"

Dealing With Money and All the Stuff You'll Need to Buy

The reality of fatherhood is sinking in. Your family and friends are looking at you differently. You feel as though things are straight between you and your partner. Some mornings you wake up feeling great and can't wait until your child joins you in the world. Other mornings you wake up with a funny taste in your mouth and your heart beating a little too hard in your chest.

In other words, things are proceeding normally.

But now that you're going to be a father, you've become aware that a certain amount of planning is in order. There are things you're going to need to buy, steps that need to be taken. The trick is not to be overwhelmed, and not to spend lavish amounts of money that you don't have in order to assuage your anxiety. The other trick is not to become a Scrooge-like tightwad, crying foul when your partner wants to buy some piece of essential baby gear. It's a tall order, but you're up for it.

PLANNING FOR THE FUTURE WITHOUT BECOMING A NEUROTIC FREAK

Suddenly you're worried all the time about money. You feel funny about spending two bucks for that cup of coffee at Starbucks. You're waiting in line at the record store, wondering whether you really *need* to spend fifteen dollars on that new Moby CD. And when you go out to buy sneakers, you come home empty-handed when you can't find anything decent for less than seventy-five bucks.

All of which is good. You're experiencing an *entirely* normal sense of apprehension, that a new era is dawning. For men, this has a great deal to do with money. No matter how much money you have, or who makes more in your domestic partnership, men feel a particular onus to somehow be fiscally *in control*. It's part of our training, from boyhood onward.

I'm not saying we're any good at actually *managing* our money, by the way. I'm terrible at it. I go as far as refusing to look at our bank statements because I don't want to know how much, or how little, money we have. As long as the bills are getting paid, I know all I need to know.

Figuring out what needs to be done in advance of your child's birth entails, like everything else about becoming a father, facing your own nature and your own limitations. Maybe you have trouble planning anything beyond what you're going to have for lunch. Or maybe your blood pressure spikes into the red zone when you entertain the very notion of moving into the future without a coherent and detailed battle plan.

Inevitably, we all revert to our selves, no matter how hard we try to be something else. Now that you're going to be a father, perhaps you think this is the time to *finally* get organized, to become a man of foresight and action. Well, it wouldn't hurt. Conversely, maybe you feel this is your moment to *finally* lighten up, to go with the flow and stop trying to control everything. This would probably also help.

But we have to be realistic. If you've always lived like a space cadet, then you're almost surely going to continue to do things like a space cadet—though maybe you can become a *slightly more effective* space cadet. And if you've always been an anal-retentive planner and inveterate list-maker, then this is probably how you're going to end up approaching this new phase of your life. Especially when things get tough. But maybe you can learn to check your excesses, and not to take your stress out on others.

Remember this concept:

YOU'RE GOING TO BE SOMEONE'S FATHER. YOU'RE ALSO STILL GOING TO BE YOURSELF— FOR BETTER OR WORSE.

When Sarah was two months pregnant, I glanced through a couple of books written for soon-to-be parents. I came away with the general impression that I was going to *have* to become a finely tuned combination of amateur midwife, psychologist, sex therapist, building engineer, and limited-portfolio investment planner. Anything short of accomplishing this goal was going to lead to my utter failure as a father and a husband, not to mention a long life of dealing with the repercussions of my myriad mistakes.

The scariest part was reading how, by the age of thirty, I should have already put money into investments. My money should have been making *more* money, rather than having been spent long ago. I needed to start thinking about my children's education—which, for the fall semester of 2016, will probably cost something like $23 million a year for a public school with in-state tuition, not including room and board.

We were doing all right, making our mortgage payments comfortably. We could afford the odd airline ticket without too much discomfort, we could take modest vacations. But this new way of looking at things was disquieting to me. I emerged from my reading and found Sarah in the living room.

"It says here we should have already been investing for years," I told her. I waved the book in the air authoritatively, as though expecting it to start explaining itself for me. "You know: 401Ks, IRAs—all that stuff."

"Sure," she agreed, looking up from her knitting. She knew I had no idea what I was talking about. *She* knew what those initials meant, but I hadn't a clue. "That's what I've been saying."

"You have?" I scratched my head and watched her hands continue with her knitting. She was working on a blanket, already preparing for the baby, while I was still trying to get my head together.

"You weren't listening to me, were you?" she asked. "I've mentioned investing our money a bunch of times. That's why I'm paying into a retirement plan at work."

"Of course I was listening," I protested. "I just hadn't . . . well . . . I mean, I never . . ."

Sarah shook her head—to her credit, with more humor than dismay. I picked up my car keys, tucked my wallet in my back pocket.

"Where are you going?" she asked.

"To take this damn book back to the library," I replied. "It's upsetting me."

Some people have all the money they need. They earn a lot of it, they have plenty in the bank, and they know all about investing it to make it work for them. More power to them.

As for the rest of us, there are options. If you have a windfall you won't need to spend for a while, you can look into short-term, low-risk investments that will at least pay more than interest in a savings account. Remember that you're going to have a lot of expenses after the baby is born, and you don't want to find yourself unable to access money you need that's locked into an investment. Make sure you know how accessible your money is at all times.

For plenty of us, the concept of extra money is laughable.

We might live from month to month. Never getting ahead. Never catching up. Try to anticipate the arrival of the baby, if possible, and the effect it will have on your budget. Plan, but don't live in a state of constant money worry. Have faith in the fact that you'll find a way to get by.

While you're at it, getting life insurance is a pretty good idea for obvious reasons. Without dwelling on the morbid, you should also prepare a will that appoints a legal guardian for your child. In the awful event that both you and your partner are dead, the will enables you to legally place your kid with the relative or friend of your choosing. You can buy a kit book for less than twenty bucks that will help you formulate your own will—if you're like us, with few real assets to sort out and bequeath, this might be the route for you (in fairness, though, the fact that Sarah is an attorney gave us added confidence in going with this low-cost route). You can also hire a lawyer to make certain that your will suits your individual estate-planning requirements, including the vital matter of guardianship.

EQUIPPING YOUR BABY: DO THEY STILL HAVE DEBTORS' PRISONS?

there's no way around it: having a baby is expensive. The question, for you, is *how* expensive. It comes down to how much money you have, and how much of it you'll be able to spend. If it helps your peace of mind, make a plan. Sit down and try to figure out your approximate income for the next year or so; don't forget to factor in your partner's maternity leave, and whether one of you might be planning to start working part-time or not at all.

Now wipe the cold sweat off your brow.

Babies need *stuff.* On the other hand, the sheer volume of stuff they actually require for their general survival and well-being is pretty flexible. They need to eat, they need clothes, and they need a warm quiet place to sleep. There are many variations within this general framework, and you'll be well served to focus on which combination suits you and your budget.

Budget is one of those laughable words, at least for a lot of people. It would be great to have a ledger of how much money comes in and how much goes out. But life has an uncanny way of getting in the way of these carefully calibrated plans. Remember: *stay flexible.*

You're probably going to be frequently tempted to spend more money on your child than you can reasonably afford. The periods before and immediately after a child's birth are times of stress and uncertainty. The inner voices are going to start up: *What have I done? How in the world am I going to pull this off?* You're going to face a few uncomfortable questions that you won't feel much like answering.

Take a deep breath. Step back. Try to smile. You're going to be fine. The baby is going to be fine. Your partner is going to be fine. Don't get locked into perpetual anxiety. To begin with, it's no fun. And it's also a dangerous state, because anxious people make bad decisions. They take action with a short-term mind-set, trying to somehow ease their worries and fill the void where their happiness should be. And one of the main traps that anxious people fall into is spending too much money.

Here's a little secret. I didn't invent it. You can find this wisdom in books, music, plays, religion, films, TV, and every other method of cultural transmission ever invented by human beings. For some reason each generation forgets this fact, and we have to relearn it again and again:

MONEY, AND THE STUFF IT BUYS, DOES NOT MAKE YOU HAPPY.

A cquiring things is not a viable long-term strategy for making yourself and those around you happy. You don't have to take it from me; just look around. Still, it's so *tempting* to go out and blow fifty bucks every time we feel bad about ourselves, or when we feel fearful about the future.

You might experience this temptation pretty strongly when you're about to become a father. There's a world of stuff out there to buy, and a lot of it is damned cool. And you'll tell yourself you're not blowing money for no reason—you're doing it for your *child*, because you want to be a good father. Somehow it all seems a lot more excusable.

A fifty-dollar jacket is not going to make a baby happy. Being with *you* is going to make the baby happy. Feeling loved is going to be the basis of her universe. And the love you find in yourself for her is where you're going to locate your real happiness.

Getting yourself in money trouble is not a good way to establish a peaceful and enjoyable family life. It can make you feel pretty exemplary to think *money is no object* when you're buying gear to set up your baby's living space. But you're not doing anyone any good if you're out there spending money you don't have.

There's a stereotype that the mother of the family is the big spender, the recreational shopper. I grew up learning gender roles from *Blondie*—the comic strip, not the group (unfortunately). The cliché is that Mom wants the best for Junior, and it's Dad's job to sweat the money. This might be true in some cases, but I suspect that as many men as women just shove all thoughts of fiscal reality deep into the recesses of their minds, in a dusty file labeled *consumer debt*.

It's understandable, and I sympathize completely. I've been there. I've spent thirty bucks on a trifle for Natasha, hoping that somehow it would make her a little happier in the future. What I didn't realize was that she would want to play with paper towels and spent deodorant dispensers.

Let me tell you: The money is going to add up *fast*. The bare necessities—diapers, bottles, formula, clothes, diaper wipes, medicine, more clothes, furniture, and various baby-safety/baby-amusement items—are going to cost tons of money even if you're carefully watching your spending. I can *guarantee* that you're going to spend more money than you thought you would, even if you're really careful.

THINGS YOUR BABY IS GOING TO NEED

3efore Natasha was born, I didn't know a bassinet from a BarcaLounger. Why should I have? It wasn't essential information.

But there are certain things that your baby will need, and which will make your transition into fatherhood easier. Being equipped in advance is a necessity. Especially if you don't have much money, because you can buy this stuff gradually—maybe an item a month throughout the pregnancy.

1. A crib or bassinet—These are what babies and small children sleep in. A bassinet is basically a basket with a hood over it. It's nice when the baby is very small, because you can keep it to the side of your bed. A crib will be necessary as the child gets a little bigger. It tends to be pretty obvious when a child is too old for a bassinet or a crib—when they get too big for it, or learn to escape it, they're ready for the next stage.

For a while you might like to have your baby sleep with you and your partner in bed. This is great. It feels cozy, and the baby is readily available for late-night feeding. Some baby-development experts say that it's good for a newborn to sleep in bed with her parents; I can't say, but I know it *feels* right. After a while, though—a month, maybe two or three—the baby gets big enough to plant a knee in your crotch in the middle of the night with the shocking force of a mule kick. Then you might be glad you have the crib. Even if the baby sleeps with you at night, it's nice to have a crib in a quiet room as a place to put the baby for naps. The sooner the baby gets used to napping in her crib, the better off you'll all be. She'll be able to sleep more peacefully, and you'll get some time off.

You're also going to need bedding: sheets, blankets, waterproof mattress pad. Don't worry about a pillow: babies don't use pillows.

🐦 **2. Clothing**—For obvious reasons. In the summer you can dress your baby in a diaper and leave it at that, but for other occasions society expects us to dress our babies in clothes. Buy clothes a size or two ahead, because babies grow fast the first year. Don't overstock on a single size. Natasha had one outfit that she outgrew between the time she was born and the time we got home from the hospital a few days later.

Remember that you're going to have to change the baby's diaper *all the time*. Pants without snaps—or at least elastic waists—for easy access are going to make you curse and throw them away.

Buy nightgowns for sleeping—they're essentially tubes with sleeves, so you can change diapers without completely undressing the baby. Think ahead in terms of how old the baby will be when the seasons change. A sundress in Minnesota in January isn't going to do anyone any good.

Buy plenty of onesies. Trust me on this one. A onesie is a T-shirt—long-sleeved or short-sleeved—that comes down under the crotch and snaps at the bottom. The snaps keep the shirt from riding up and exposing your baby's belly. It is the king of all baby clothes—lightweight, versatile, perfect as an inner layer or on its own in warm weather.

Dress the baby warmly. She can't move around much, so she doesn't generate her own body heat the way we do. A good cold-weather safety test is to check her naked belly under her clothes—she should be nice and toasty. Then check her toes and fingers—her extremities should be cooler than her belly, but still reasonably warm.

A frightening number of your baby's clothes come with some sort of stitched insignia emblazoned on the chest, right over the heart: teddy bears, rabbits, kittens, crude renderings of rattles and balls. I think the nebulous powers that manufacture these garments are adding these features to create uniforms for a baby army. When the call to arms comes, we unsuspecting parents will find out that our children have been living secret lives as members of the Puppy Platoon and the Bunny Battalion. Think about *that* the next time you're putting Junior into his sleeper suit.

3. Infant car seat—You need one of these even if you don't own a car. Eventually you're going to take your infant someplace in an auto. Hospitals are required by law to make sure you have a working car seat before allowing you to take the baby home. You might think this is a pain in the ass—if you're the kind of cowboy who still gets chafed about having to wear a seat belt. Make sure you buy the right kind of car seat—rear-facing—and put it in the backseat of your car like the instructions tell you to.

Infant car seats come with handles, so you can snap them out and carry them around. I always found this to be more trouble than it was worth. You'll be all right with this first car seat, generally speaking, until your baby weighs about twenty pounds or more.

4. Feeding supplies—This means bottles, nipples, and baby formula. Even if your partner is going to breast-feed, you're going to need these supplies on hand as a backup. What if your partner is stuck in traffic and the baby is squawking like a pterodactyl? You can usually find a starter kit that contains everything you're going to need at first—and you'll probably get some supplies free from the hospital. Even if your child is going to be breast-fed, it's a good idea to keep a tub of formula on hand in case of emergencies.

🐚 **5. Changing table**—This is optional—sort of. Just keep in mind that you're going to be changing about ten diapers a day at first. You're going to want a space devoted to diaper changing—a place where, ideally, you can stand comfortably while you work, and where all your supplies are within reach. Changing a diaper on the sofa once or twice is fine, but eventually you're going to get involved with a very messy diaper—and you're going to want it all to go down onto a washable pad and not onto upholstery. If you have enough space in your home, you can buy a fairly cheap changing table with drawers underneath where you can keep your baby's clothes. Another possibility is putting a pad down on a bureau and making do with that. A good changing table also comes with a guardrail and a little seat belt, so you can strap the baby in while you rummage around underneath for a clean onesie. But remember not to leave her unattended on the changing table—that's just asking for trouble.

🐚 **6. A mode of travel**—You'll need to get around with your baby, and she'll start to feel heavy in your arms before too long. There are two main ways of toting a baby around: on your body or on wheels. You can find a pack that enables you to carry your baby hands-free on your chest, which works well while they're small. Your other option is the stroller, which babies tend to like because of the lulling effects of motion. There are many strollers to choose from, so consider what you need. Thicker wheels are better for maneuverability, while some models are designed for joggers. Test out a collapsible model by breaking it down and trying to carry it—some strollers are heavy and pretty unwieldy. If you're strapped for money, remember that cheaper models work just fine.

Your baby will probably *love* her stroller or her Snugli-style front pack. You'll go for long walks together, you'll take her to the supermarket and the bookstore in mutual bliss. She'll take naps while you both enjoy sunshine and fresh air. But then one day the joy will be gone. She'll cry and struggle in what was once a happy, cozy confine.

You'll wonder why your paradise has been snatched away from you. But not if you know what's going on well in advance.

This is where your troubleshooting skills will come in handy. Natasha suddenly became miserable in both her Snugli and her stroller, turning relaxing walks into anxiety-ridden crying festivals. Turns out she had gotten bigger and didn't like the way she was arranged—lying down in the stroller, and facing my chest in the Snugli. I adjusted the stroller into a sitting position, and turned her around in the Snugli so she was facing out and could see her environment. And she was happy again. Be prepared for change, and you'll both be a lot happier.

7. **Lots of rags**—Your baby is going to throw up a lot. Don't worry, it's not that bad. Usually it's just a little partially digested milk, and it doesn't take long before you're used to wiping streaks of it off your shoulder. It's a good idea to have a supply of rags for wiping up little messes: we bought about a dozen cheap cloth diapers to use for this purpose.

8. **Baby blankets**—Having a few small baby blankets on hand will enable you to keep the baby warm and to create a little bundle out of her when you need to step outside with her to get the mail. A nurse at the hospital will teach you how to swaddle the baby, which essentially means wrapping her up like a cigar. Within a week or two she won't like it anymore, so enjoy it while you can.

BUT THIS WILL COST MORE THAN A SPACE SHUTTLE LAUNCH

 i know. Here are some money-saving ideas to help cushion the blow:

🐌 **1. Cloth diapers**—Cloth diapers are a one-time investment of about a dollar apiece, and they're reusable indefinitely. You also have to buy diaper wraps, which enable you to Velcro together the diaper into a viable liquid/solid retainment device. Setting up this system can save you a lot of money otherwise spent on disposable diapers. The downside is that you have to clean the diapers in a washing machine—or by hand, if you have the temperament of a nineteenth-century Old West settler. By the time the baby is about four or five months old, you'll have to dump messy diapers in the toilet before tossing them in the bin for washing. It's not an appetizing prospect, but the savings are considerable. We gave up on cloth diapers when Natasha was about six months old—it simply got too gross—and shifted entirely to disposables. Also be wary of buying the cheapest disposable diapers on the shelf—I've heard horror stories from other parents about fasteners coming loose and resulting in severe leakage.

🐌 **2. Breast-feeding**—Breast-feeding saves tons of money on powdered baby formula, which costs about twenty bucks for a tub that might last less than a week. Some women choose not to breast-feed, and for others logistical considerations preclude it. There are pumps available for working mothers to stockpile breast milk, if they decide to go that route. Eventually even breast-fed babies tend to require formula as a dietary supplement.

🐌 **3. Medicine**—This means gas medicine, Infants' Tylenol for fevers, diaper-rash cream, and teething ointment. Not everyone wishes to use all of these medicines, although I gave them all to Natasha at various times and they seemed to help. You can buy generic equivalents of these, and other over-the-counter baby medications, at decent drugstores. Some health-care providers run in-house pharmacies at their clinics, where they sell medicine at slightly lower prices to members.

🐚 **4. Thrift stores/outlet stores**—Babies wear clothes for only a little while before they grow out of them. It doesn't make much sense to spend money you don't have on baby clothes. With a little energy you can find deals at secondhand stores and sales at national chains like Target and Kmart. With a little more effort, you can find changing tables, bedding, and strollers at thrift shops or even garage sales for a lot less than you would pay for the same items brand-new. (Cribs are dicier—some older models have been deemed unsafe.) The same can be true of discount outlet stores, although I've found that at times their prices aren't really that much less than retail. If you're worried about money, comparison-shop before laying your money down.

🐚 **5. Family members**—I don't recommend turning into an inveterate sponge living off your nearest and dearest, but don't underestimate how much your family wants to help out. If they express a desire to buy your baby a nice gift, offer a few suggestions. It's better to get a nice comforter for the baby's crib than to receive another stuffed panda bear to throw on the pile.

🐚 **6. Other parents**—If you know any other parents with small children, or who once had small children, communicate with them. Pretty soon you'll meet someone with a child even younger than yours, and then you'll see how most parents like to help other parents out. You might be able to borrow a stroller or a bag of outgrown baby clothes, with a promise to eventually return the stuff when your baby is done with it. We borrowed a saucer contraption from Sarah's coworker Laura, which enabled

Natasha to rest suspended in a standing position—it was Natasha's favorite Teletubbies-viewing spot for months. Sarah's sister Eva sent us two boxes of outgrown baby clothes that had belonged to her two daughters, saving us from untold expense.

Of course, the best way to save money is not to spend it. It helped both Sarah and me to keep in mind how little our parents possessed materially when we were babies, and how everything worked out just fine. You can't scrimp on the essentials, but there's also no good reason to run up a couple thousand bucks on your Visa card because you wanted to set up the *perfect* room for your baby. Babies don't know much about their surroundings. They want to be warm, well fed, secure, and loved. These things don't have to cost much money. Just remember that a year of college in 2016 is going to cost $23 million!

IN THE WILDS OF BABYLAND

Let's say you have a couple hundred bucks in the bank, and you're setting up your baby's sleeping space. You want to get a nice crib—not necessarily a four-poster with a gauzy overhang and silk sheets, but something comfortable and serviceable for the next two years. Something that, eventually, you could reuse for your next child or children.

Shudder. Excuse me. I shouldn't have brought up that topic.

You get in the car, hit the freeway, and head out for the suburbs. That's where all the big stores are located, on the horizon at the head of those endless parking lots. We're talking about the mega–sporting goods store with the indoor basketball court and batting cage. The mega–pet store with Himalayan mounds of kitty litter and epicurean selections of dog biscuits. The mega–electronics store with enough technological hardware to run the Death Star.

And, of course, the mega–baby store. *Shudder.*

You walk in the door. Babies, babies, babies. And more babies. Pregnant women. Anxious men. Soft piped-in music, lost and distorted in the high plastic-foam ceiling. Countless rows of merchandise. A wave of pastel pinks and blues washing over your field of vision.

I went to a place like this. First it filled me with an overpowering sense of doom. I thought, *Man, I could really lose my shirt in here.*

Racks and racks of baby clothes. *Don't even look at the price tags.* Twenty-five varieties of infant car seats. Galaxies of baby-safety products. A universe of strollers . . . My *God,* who would have ever imagined there were so many different kinds of strollers?

Price cards beneath each item included two figures—a theoretical retail price, and your lower price to indicate how much money you were "saving." As though it was a *privilege* to come in there and spend your last cent.

"You want to know something?" I said, halting and raising a censorious finger in the air.

"What?" Sarah asked, made somewhat nervous by my tone, and the fact that we'd only gotten ten feet from the front door. She didn't care much for this place either, but she lacked the Y chromosome that made the mega-store anathema to the male constitution.

"Look at this price tag. It *says* you're getting a discount." I pointed at a baby backpack as though I'd never seen anything so ridiculous in my life. "But who says it's the truth? I'll bet they're making it all up. They artificially inflate the prices, then pretend to mark them down. It's a *scam,* I'm telling you."

"Come on," she said, exasperated already. "Let's get what we came for. Then we can leave."

"Suit yourself," I muttered. "But I want to go on record as saying that I have a *very bad feeling* about this place."

We were accompanied by Sarah's father and his wife, Betty,

who had generously offered to buy us a crib. In the crib-and-bed section my foreboding deepened.

There were cribs everywhere. Big cribs, little cribs, fancy cribs, plain cribs. What did *I* know about cribs? How should *I* know what crib we should buy? I didn't even remember *sleeping* in a crib. Who did? Why couldn't the baby sleep in a dresser drawer like something in a Steinbeck novel? Wouldn't there be a certain *charm* to that? Well, *wouldn't* there?

The tension was ratcheted up another notch when we narrowed our selections. There was a question whether or not that item we really wanted would be in stock.

"Bait and switch!" I crowed. "I *knew* it!"

"Well, they're saying we can pay now and come back when they have the crib in stock," Jeff explained, typically unflappable. "You'll have plenty of time to get it set up before the baby is born."

I glowered. But wasn't that what *they* wanted? Wasn't that how the trap was set?

Finally we sat down with a very competent and pleasant woman who tried to sell us the crib we had selected at a very reasonable price. For no reason at all, and to a degree that was somehow beyond my control, I became very difficult to deal with.

"That's all well and good," I said with the bitterness of a man who *knew* he was being taken to the cleaners. "But this crib is very big. How am I supposed to get it home? Can you tell me that?"

"Oh, it's no problem," the saleswoman explained. "We do it all the time. What kind of car do you drive?"

"A Subaru four-door," I replied cautiously, like a man sitting under the hot lights of a police interrogation.

She smiled. "You can push down the backseat and slide the box through the trunk. We do it all the time. It's never a problem."

"Never a problem," I repeated under my breath, my hostility mounting. "Well, my car *doesn't do that.*"

"Look, Quinton," Jeff said. "I'll give you some money and you can rent a truck if you need to. It's not a big deal."

I looked around. I had no allies. I wanted to shout: *We're ruined! Am I the only one who can see things as they really are? We were finished as soon as we set foot inside this place!*

My tormentors then ushered me to the checkout line with the expediency of a group of orderlies shepherding a mental patient let loose on a day-pass. While we waited in line I remembered something my friend Gary had told me. Gary's partner Julie was expecting a child a few months after ours. He had come to a mega-store just like this one. The atmosphere had gotten to him, too. Finally he had cracked and refused to give his zip code to the cashier who wanted to ring up their purchases.

We moved closer to the front of the line. I felt a sense of admiration for Gary's fortitude. He had made it almost to the end before breaking down. I had lost it back in the crib section.

We reached the cashier.

"Your zip code?" she asked, the first words out of her mouth. Sarah recited ours.

"This is where they got to Gary," I muttered.

Sarah looked up. "Excuse me?" she asked.

"Nothing." I sighed. "I think it's time for me to go home."

So when you find yourself in the mega–baby store, a parallel universe of pink and baby blue, an unearthly realm of mobiles and toys, try to *chill out*. If you can. Just be prepared for that zip-code part. A good man went down there, just when he was about to make a clean escape.

4

The Home Stretch

Birthing Class, Picking Names, and
Preparing for the Delivery

After a while the ostrich method of dealing with your
impending fatherhood will start to break down.
There are too many hands tugging at your feathers,
urging you to come up into the sunlight and deal
with what's going on. You have to start confronting
reality. I *know* I recommended the ostrich method,
and I know how hard it is to let it go. But it was nice
while it lasted, wasn't it?

Your partner's belly is getting bigger every day,
or so it seems. She might have had an ultrasound. It's
time to pick out names, plan for the delivery, and
maybe start a birthing class. You've circled the due
date on your calendar with a Magic Marker. You're
having visions of delivery rooms and doctors spanking
red newborn bottoms. It's *coming*. Be strong. Keep
doing those deep-breathing exercises, and keep living
your life. Take it from me: it's going to be fine.

SO WHAT'S WRONG WITH DAFFODIL MOONFLOWER?

W hat's in a name?

Well, there's the future playground teasing, for one thing. And it's one thing to be open-minded and progressive, but is Daffodil Moonflower really such a great name for a boy?

From the time you learned you were going to be parents, you and your partner have undoubtedly been talking about what you're going to name your child. Hopefully this has been a healthy give-and-take and not a fractious free-for-all. Some couples find it extremely easy to name their children; for others the process is a battle of wills.

You should do your part to ensure that naming your child doesn't devolve into an argument that will always symbolize every disagreement you've ever had with your partner. If you like Charles and she likes Jack, try to find a compromise. Try talking to the baby in Mom's belly for a few days, trying on names for size until one sounds right.

If you're stumped, check out a book of names from the library—but be warned, there are thousands, and you might get overwhelmed. Make a list of your favorites and her favorites, and allow each other two or three vetoes as you winnow the list down.

Sometimes people get attached to family names and wish to pass them down to their children. Try not to dig in your heels and become obstinate. Remember, Aloysius can always be shortened to Al. By the same token, be careful when you're discussing this process with friends. Invariably someone is going to have an Uncle Clifton—and might *not* have a sense of humor about what a bad name you think it is.

In our case, the name we chose reflected the time of the baby's birth. As you know, my child was conceived after I returned from a weeklong trip to St. Petersburg, where a woman named Natasha had given a friend and me a tour of the Hermitage, expertly leading us to the museum's greatest treasures in the small amount of free time we had carved out of our schedule. I liked the name Natasha, and Sarah agreed it seemed a natural for our daughter. Now, of course, we can't imagine her being named anything else.

The matter of surnames is usually pretty straightforward, although of course some women keep their own names when they get married. I personally think bestowing a hyphenated, compromise surname on your child is pretty ridiculous—what if they marry someone else with this kind of name and have a child? Is their child going to have *four* last names? But ultimately it's a personal choice, and no harm is done either way.

We chose an unorthodox solution. Sarah wanted Natasha to have her last name, which she'd kept when we were married in 1991. We gave Natasha the middle name Jane, with my surname as a second middle name. I know that from here on out I'm going to have to field well-meaning questions: *Are you Natasha's stepfather? Are you and Sarah married?* But I can handle it. We did things a little differently because we wanted to. Answering a few questions along the way is a small price to pay.

FINDING OUT THE BABY'S GENDER

Depending on your insurance coverage and how your partner's pregnancy is progressing, she might make an appointment for an ultrasound examination. An ultrasound involves waving a weird sort of sonar wand over the pregnant woman's belly while cool deep-sea sound effects come out of a big box. You look at a screen and see a black-and-white image of the baby in the womb.

It's extremely cool, and you might find yourself deeply affected emotionally by the first sight of your child. I know I was. Natasha was just a few months into her gestation, but the ultrasound technician was able to point out her spine and beating heart to Sarah and me. The baby was *alive*. These tests are excellent because they help assuage your fears that something might be wrong with the child.

Natasha was too young during the first ultrasound for the technician to determine her gender; she was also in a demure position in the womb that didn't allow us a good look at her private parts. But several months later we went back for another test, and the technician looked up from her screen with an expectant expression.

"Do you want to know the sex of the baby?" she asked.

"Yes," I said.

"No," Sarah said simultaneously.

We looked at each other. *Oops.* Turns out we hadn't discussed the subject in advance.

Fortunately we laughed together about our misunderstanding. Sarah shrugged. "OK, why not?" she said. I guess sitting on a table with jelly smeared all over her belly and sonar waves exposing her insides had made her feel she had little to lose.

I *like* information. I want to know everything there is to know—including the gender of my unborn child. I figured that knowing her gender would help me to think of her as a real person, and that I would be better prepared when she was born.

Some people don't want to know the sex of the baby in advance. There are good reasons for this—they want to be surprised; they want the moment of birth to be like the unveiling of a mystery. I understand this, but I can't go along for the ride. I was the kid shaking the presents on Christmas Eve, separating the books from the toys.

"It's a girl," the technician said. She pointed at Natasha's genitalia on the screen. "See?"

"Yeah," I said. "I know what *that* is."

Sarah shot me a look.

I took her hand and felt tears warming my eyes. A girl. My daughter. Our daughter. The technician turned the wand and we saw her face. She had bowed lips, almond-shaped eyes that were closed in sleep. I had never in my life seen anything so beautiful.

Mystery is fine. But give me knowledge any day. Seeing Natasha on that ultrasound screen and knowing she was going to be a little girl was one of the greatest moments in my life.

But not everyone is going to feel the same way. Discuss the matter with your partner before you go in for the test. Respect her wishes if she feels strongly either way. If she wants to wait, that's all right. You'll find out soon enough.

And you won't have an ultrasound technician looking at you with an expression that asks: *You two are married, right? It's not one of those green-card, only-met-once-or-twice deals, is it?*

BIRTHING CLASS: VALUABLE RESOURCE OR UNENDURABLE TRIAL?

When your partner is well into her second trimester you'll have to decide whether or not to attend a birthing class for first-time parents. Usually these classes are set up by your health-care provider, although you can also find classes through county services if your insurance doesn't offer them.

Our birthing class met every Wednesday night for six weeks, three hours per class. That's eighteen hours to you and me. That's a *long time* to spend watching videos of women giving birth and doing Kegel exercises.

You might be tempted to blow off the class. Maybe, like me, you'd had enough of school when you graduated from college, thank you very much. You might think that you could spend those eighteen hours in a more enjoyable fashion—say, watching the Knicks play the Spurs on TV.

Sorry, but you should go. Your partner will probably want to attend, and you wouldn't want her to be the only mother there without a spouse. It's bad for the image.

Here's the valuable information that you are going to glean from your birthing class: *Your partner is going to have a baby pretty soon.* If, like me, you were clinging to the ostrich method of fatherhood, this will provide the shock to prod you out of your complacency. She's not just getting wide in the middle, man, she's going to *give birth*.

Birthing class forced me to confront my imminent fatherhood in a structured setting. I got to watch other fathers face the same heavy reality. I got used to the idea by going through the birthing process in excruciating detail. In the bargain, I was gradually desensitized. By the time they were done with me, something had clicked in my mind. I was finally able to think about the baby without breaking out in flopsweat.

MY PEERS, THESE PARENTS

remember high school? You probably don't want to, but indulge me. Remember the first day, how you found yourself surrounded by people you would never hang out with if it wasn't *against the law* for you to get up and leave? The first night of birthing class has a similar feel. Except all the women are pregnant, instead of one or two. And all the men look a little queasy.

Our birthing class was held at the hospital where Natasha would eventually be born. We took the elevator down to the basement, walked past the cafeteria (which was closed, damn it: I could have gone for a plate of hospital noodles or a leathery cutlet—birthing class gave me anxiety hunger). We ended up in a conference room with cheap carpeting and a low ceiling. We filled out name tags and sat in a circle with the other couples.

Everybody seemed pretty chipper at first. There was fear in the men's eyes, but that was only natural. It was a strange scene, with all the distended bellies. And *then* there were the mothers.

We dove right in. Our teacher, Susie, had one kid, and she was optimistic and humorous about all the parenthood that was about to explode all around us. The first order of business was each of us telling the group what we were most worried about.

I knew what I was worried about. I was extremely worried about the fact that *my wife was going to have a baby*. No one brought this up, though, and I realized that I was going to have to get more specific.

"I'm scared of the pain of delivery," one woman said. Which was rational enough.

"I'm worried about being a good father," said a quiet guy in glasses and a thick beard.

My turn came. I told the group that I was having a recurring dream about a baby crying, which was true. A few times I had woken in the night and looked around for the baby. I also said that I was generally anxious about making ends meet, and about providing a good material life for my daughter. The other men nodded somberly.

Susie pulled down a screen. It was movie time. I felt heavy-lidded and sleepy, until the video began.

The couple in the video were real anal-retentive types, it seemed to me. The father was getting on my nerves: he was pro-grammatic, and his exhortations to his wife during delivery seemed too aggressive. Then the baby was born and my heart melted. By the time it was over I was wiping tears from my face. I hoped with all my heart that the couple ended up having a good life together, and that their child was healthy and happy.

Whew. That was intense.

"What did you think?" Sarah asked.

"It was fine," I croaked.

By the second Wednesday we were very deep into various stages of the childbirth process. Think about it: Do you know anything about the nuts and bolts of how a child is born—the different phases and the way they can play out? Of course you don't. Why should you? The good news is that you can learn everything in about an hour.

Time for another movie. *Oh, no.* This time the birth was harder; there was a lot of pain and blood. I looked around the circle. Men and women alike were squirming, their mouths agape. By the time it was over I was crying again. I rubbed my eyes and cleared my throat, tried to get myself together for when the lights came up.

Susie talked about all the things that can go wrong. She passed around pictures of various benign problems that babies can experience during the first few days of their lives.

You might have spent some time perusing baby books and magazines, looking at little cherubic creatures dressed in adorable outfits. Well, chances are the children you're looking at aren't newborns.

Here's a little secret. A lot of newborns are *ugly*. In our birthing class we were given shock therapy in the form of a series of snapshots depicting newborns in various degrees of ugliness. Don't be shocked in the delivery room if your child looks more like Yoda than the rosy-cheeked vision of your dreams.

There are a lot of reasons for this. Some children, during the trauma of birth, get marks on their heads and face. My daughter had a red splotch on her forehead that took more than a year to disappear. Other kids come out with skin conditions such as wrinkling, scales, marks, and general hideousness.

Don't fret. Almost all of this will go away before you even get home from the hospital after your forty-eight-hour stay. It won't be like the episode of *Seinfeld* where Jerry and Elaine have to put their hands over their mouths to keep from vomiting at the sight of their friends' infant son.

Other newborns are, well, kind of ugly anyway. They have scrunched-up little faces, scowls, bulging foreheads, bug eyes. Remember, they're infants. They're going to grow up fast and look better a lot sooner than you might think. Just be prepared. Anyway, no matter what your child looks like at first, I guarantee you're going to think she's the most beautiful thing you've ever seen.

My personal low point was reached when Susie started to describe the surgical tongs used as a last-ditch strategy for pulling a reluctant baby out of its mother.

"If they're using the tongs," she explained, turning serious, "then things aren't going very well at all."

"Noted," I whispered. I put down my sugar cookie, which had suddenly lost its appeal.

We broke off into two groups, men on one side of the room and women on the other. We made lists of things we were worried about—not that they had changed much from the first night. But we saw more clearly that the fathers and mothers were worried about different things. Oh, and that the fathers were basically foolish and ridiculous. I already knew *that,* so I didn't think the exercise helped me much.

More videos. Lots of blood. Grunting. Screaming. One of the mothers was fearful and anxious about giving birth; by this point she was lying on a pillow on the floor, squirming and groaning. I felt very sorry for her. I glanced around the room as one video recorded an intense and difficult delivery. All of the fathers-to-be were staring at the screen goggle-eyed and anxious.

We launched into breathing exercises, which are supposed to help women while giving birth. I paid close attention, ready to be a coach if called upon. *Breathe through the pain,* Susie told us. Remember, it's pain for a purpose, and it won't last forever.

Picture twenty adults panting in unison. *Pant pant pant. Hee hee hee. Pant pant pant.*

As the weeks passed I realized that I was starting to look forward to Wednesday night. Birthing class had demystified what lay ahead, and enabled me to look forward to the birth of my daughter with clear vision and a sense of reality. I was ready. I couldn't wait.

This is the point *you* need to reach. Because there's no turning back.

Not everyone responds so well to birthing classes. My friend

Kevan went to one birthing class and basically laughed behind his hand the whole time. Then he left early. Kevan is the kind of guy who learns things on his own, and he's rarely unprepared for what life throws at him.

I'm not like that. I avoid dealing with big scary matters until I'm forced to take some action. Birthing class is made for people like me, who need to be eased into major changes.

If you plan to assist your partner with her delivery, a birthing class will teach you what you need to know. Then, in all likelihood, you can forget everything they taught you and simply hold her hand, offer encouragement, and be there for her. The important thing is that you feel ready, prepared, and forewarned. A good class will take you through the process from start to finish—including where you can park your car when you arrive, an issue that nagged at me. Listen closely, then relax.

It's going to happen soon. It's scary, and it's wonderful. Take my word for it: the birth of your child will be a day you never forget, and I'd bet money that you'll remember it as the best day of your life.

You should have a frank discussion with your partner about her strategy for dealing with the pain of labor—we're talking drugs here. If for no other reason, you need to know how she feels in case anyone at the hospital asks you.

There are a few options available, and they vary depending on the hospital. The strongest medicine is an *epidural*, which is shot into the spine and basically numbs the woman from the waist down. It curbs the pain, but it also may make it difficult to push the baby out because the muscles required are cut off from sensation. You can also request lighter painkillers—essentially opiates. There are risks and side effects, which you should both discuss with your doctor or midwife.

Don't be judgmental about your partner's decision. After all, *she's* the one who's going to have a baby. And keep in mind that she can change her mind after she gets to the hospital—up to a point in the delivery after which no drugs can be administered. Understand her plan, stand by her, and remind her that she's strong enough to get through it.

TO BE THERE OR NOT TO BE THERE

One of the biggest questions you have to answer now is how you and your partner are going to handle the delivery of your child.

If you plan, like most men today, to be in the delivery room, the general advice for how to handle it is simple: *do what seems right*. You may have learned some simple breathing exercises in birthing class to help your partner through her contractions, but let her take the lead. Don't be a boss; don't try to usher her through the experience unless she asks you to. I know your heart is in the right place, but put yourself in her position. *She* will know what she needs—just make sure you listen to her, and offer constant support and praise. Nearly every man who has taken part in a delivery will agree that his job was simply to be a part of things.

There are a few different options for approaching childbirth that have become more popular in the last decade. Discuss options with your partner and ask about your insurance coverage— you might have more options than you think.

A traditional birth involves a doctor and nurses. Typically the doctor won't get involved until the actual birth is imminent. A second option involves a *midwife,* who is a trained professional specializing in childbirth. A midwife may or may not be a registered nurse. For most midwife deliveries, a doctor won't get involved unless there are complications. A third wrinkle is the *doula,* who specializes in assisting the mother and meeting the mother's needs during and immediately after the birth. A doula doesn't replace a doctor or midwife, but focuses on easing and enhancing the mother's experience of birth.

For many couples, there's no question that the expectant dad is going to be there the entire time, as a coach, observer, or general source of encouragement. It's the norm today, and it's viewed as an act of support and compassion on the part of the man—who, of course, is exempt from the actual birthing process but can cheer on from the sidelines.

The fathers I've talked to about being in the delivery room express a range of feelings. Some found it difficult, yet for many others it was a defining event in their lives that they wouldn't trade for the world. Most of all, it's an intensely private and personal experience between the man and his partner—and, in some cases, friends and family—when they welcome their child into the world together.

The arrangement in the birthing room should be determined by the mother-to-be. It's her party, and she should invite the guests. Sit down with your partner and ask her what she really wants. Don't pressure her about it and don't play games. Delivering a child is beautiful and life-changing, but it's also painful hard work. The mother should feel free to express her needs about how the actual birth should go down. If she wants you on her right, you're there. Or her left. If she wants you on both sides at the same time, try to figure out a way to make it happen.

For some people, the best option might be for the father *not* to be in the delivery room, although it goes against the grain of today's expectations to even raise this question. The (sometimes) unspoken assumption is that you were eager enough to be there for the fun part, so there's no way you're going to get off the hook for the messy conclusion. It's your right as well as your obligation. It's something you shouldn't even *think* about not doing.

Things were different when we were born. Parents on the more progressive (i.e., hippie) end of the social scale started to include the father in the birthing process. Children from more working-class backgrounds, such as myself, were born in hospitals while our mothers were basically numbed by large doses of drugs. Our fathers were in the waiting room watching *Laugh-In*, or watching Richard Nixon sweat his way through a speech. If the father wanted to come into the birthing room and take part, well, that was probably all right. Long hair, psychedelic music, can't tell the girls from the boys . . . the kids were into a lot of strange things in those days.

Over time, conventions changed. The progressive viewpoint—placing the father squarely in the delivery room—became more of a norm. Many things in American society changed in the sixties—a lot of them very enlightened and sensible, resulting in the betterment of our society. The father's involvement in childbirth was one such case. If you want to be there, you shouldn't have to explain yourself or feel unwanted.

In our childbirth-education class of about ten couples, *every single one* of the fathers planned to be in the delivery room for the birth of his child.

Except me.

I didn't have the guts to tell this to the class. In that atmosphere, I feared they would have taken down my name and address and passed it on to Child Protective Services. *We'd better keep an eye on this one. He's not going to be in the delivery room? God knows what else he's going to be capable of. He'll probably keep the baby in a footlocker and only let it out once a day for bread and water.*

Having a child makes you aware of social norms and pressures that you didn't know existed. Until Natasha was conceived, I had no idea that men were *expected* to be in the delivery room during birth.

And that they were supposed to *like* it. No, *love* it. It's supposed to be such a special thing, one of the great experiences of every *good* man's life.

Let me ask you this: Have you ever seen a child being born? I have. It was miraculous, absolutely incredible. I cried tears of happiness for a couple I'd never even met, for an event that must have happened years ago.

But it was also bloody, impossibly intimate, and more than a little gross.

There. I said it. Those of you who want to throw rocks at my head, go ahead and get in line. But don't get me wrong. It's easy to misinterpret what I'm saying, but give me the benefit of hearing me out:

IF YOU WANT TO BE IN THE DELIVERY ROOM, BY ALL MEANS BE THERE. IT WILL BE AN ASTONISHING EXPERIENCE.

AND IF YOUR PARTNER WANTS YOU THERE, DON'T EVEN THINK ABOUT WEASELING OUT OF IT. YOUR PRESENCE IS MANDATORY.

Natasha's birth was the best day of my life. It changed and broadened my life and soul in ways that I am still discovering. I love my wife more than ever before, and I love and treasure Natasha so much that it almost cheapens my feelings to describe them in words.

But I didn't want to see her being born.

It's not that I can't stand the sight of blood. As research for a writing project, I've gone into operating rooms and seen surgical procedures. I don't like blood, but I'm a big boy and I can take it. The pain and suffering of a loved one, though, is an entirely different matter. When Sarah once cut her finger while cooking and had to get stitches in the emergency room, I was almost on the floor. The doctor was more worried about me than about her. I felt an overpowering empathy for Sarah—not to mention a sense of profound helplessness—that was almost enough to make me pass out.

This was a major factor in our decision. I had a hard time with the prospect of watching Sarah suffer without being able to do anything to help. Childbirth is beautiful, but it also involved pain and suffering.

Let's be clear: If Sarah had expressed a strong desire for my presence in the delivery room, then *I damned well would have been there*. I told her explicitly that if, at any point, she changed her mind and wanted me there, then all she had to do was say the word: I'd jump in wholeheartedly and do everything that was required of me.

Sarah, however, didn't want it. My lack of enthusiasm was surely a major factor in *her* decision, but there was more to it, and her rationale deserves consideration.

She knew labor was probably going to be the hardest thing she would ever endure, but she also knew she was going to meet the challenge. And she understood in advance how she would deal with the pain—by going inside herself. When she gets a bad case of the flu, she holes up in a dark room and suffers in privacy. For her, sickness and pain are best experienced alone, without fanfare.

She told me that when things got intense during labor, the last thing she wanted was to have to worry about how I was doing, or even to deal with me *in any way*. We have a very close connection, and she knew that her concern for *my* well-being would take away her focus from the job at hand. She knew she was going to be in a safe place during labor—with a nurse and a midwife helping her every step of the way—and she felt that she could derive the most strength from forging a bond with these women. She could behave any way she wanted around them without worrying what they thought—or, worse, having it captured on videotape. She could get through the pain without having to be self-conscious.

At first her midwife looked skeptically at me upon learning

that I wasn't going to stay in the birthing room. After Natasha was born, she softened on the subject. The midwife told Sarah how, when *she* was having her child, her husband wanted to watch a football game on TV during labor. She had positioned her husband so that he could watch the TV while seeming to focus on her face—because she was worried about what the nurses would think.

Some people choose to take pictures or shoot video in the birthing room during labor and delivery. They end up with a document of the day that they can look at with warmth and pride. Or else they have an embarrassing video that Mom never wants to see again.

If you're going to wield a camera in the birthing room, tackle the assignment as if you were the director of a major film. Sit down with your star and ask her how she would like to be filmed. From the waist up only? Or would she like a full, no-holds-barred documentary? Would she prefer the cameras to be turned off during contractions, or does she want a souvenir of her trials to remember always?

Think it through with your partner in advance, and you'll have a happier cast and a better film. And act fast when she tells you to *put that damned camera away.*

THE BEST WAY IS YOUR WAY

his is the key to remember: find out how your partner wants to handle labor and childbirth, honor her wishes, and proceed accordingly. There is no right way, no wrong way—and ignore anyone who tells you otherwise.

Giving birth to a baby is an act of incredible bravery. Any woman who does it should be applauded and recognized as a complete *bad-ass*. Often I think having children is what makes women stronger than men. And for many women, having their partner present is a crucial part of the process. Their partner grounds them, gives them strength, and pulls them back to shore when the pain becomes overwhelming.

Given our times, your partner will probably want you in the delivery room. In that case you have to be there, and you have to give it your all. It will be an event that you'll remember forever, and you'll be glad that you were there when she needed you. If your partner thinks she'd be better off without you, be ready to meet your child when she finally comes into the world.

After Natasha was born, Sarah told other mothers how we handled the delivery. Invariably, at first they were surprised. The father's absence from the birthing room suggests, in today's culture, all sorts of unsavory motivations: *he doesn't care, he's selfish, he left her to suffer alone.*

But then, after they've really thought about it, a surprising number of mothers have told Sarah that they would have liked to have done it the same way. Because, frankly, many men are deadweight in the delivery room. The mother ends up worrying about her partner at the precise moment when she should be focusing on nothing but herself and birthing the child.

Many, many other women would not agree. They want their partner there for a variety of reasons—and, in the end, they shouldn't have to explain themselves. Their wishes are the law in this case. Make sure you know what your partner wants. And make sure she understands that you'll do anything for her.

5

Hello, Daddy

Preparing for the Hospital, My Story, and What
Happens Just After Your Child Is Born

The final weeks before the birth of your child are
likely to be pretty tough. Your partner is going to be
uncomfortable: her joints will ache, she'll be tired,
and the size of her belly will make it hard for her to
sit, stand, or lie down.

All you can really do is offer sympathy and
support. And don't get offended when she demands
to know *what the hell* do you know about it, you
wouldn't last for *an hour* with this giant creature inside you. She's probably right. I know it would be
hard for me to maintain a consistently sunny outlook
if I was carrying a full-term baby.

The truth is, it's no picnic for *you*, either. The
pregnancy so far, if things have gone well, has been
fairly cushy. You've had plenty of time to get used to
thinking about the changes that are coming. But now
those changes are actually going to happen, and your
boat is about to be rocked. Big time.

Talk about your feelings with your partner if it makes you feel better. But also keep in mind that sometimes it's better to stay mum. It's great to talk about how much you're looking forward to meeting and holding your child. But your partner probably doesn't want to hear about how frightened and anxious you might feel. Calm, steady, and confident are the words of the day. Offer your support by keeping your head on straight.

THE END OF THE LINE

In Sarah's eighth month of pregnancy she couldn't get comfortable in bed to sleep. She tossed and turned, cursed under her breath, and woke up every couple of hours. Fortunately we have a guest room. One night I picked up my pillow and my book, said a few kind words, and decamped for more peaceful quarters down the hall. I left her with our bed to herself, so she didn't have to worry about waking me. I think I got the better of the deal, though. During those last couple of weeks I got the best sleep that I would enjoy for almost a full year.

Finally Sarah had carried Natasha to the first of December, the baby's due date. And nothing happened.

"Weren't you supposed to have had that baby already?" I asked.

"*Very funny,*" she replied.

We began an around-the-clock wait. From the looks of it, I didn't think Sarah could get much bigger. She started to talk all the time about how much she *wanted* to give birth. She wanted the baby out of her, she wanted to hold it and care for it.

"Come on, Natasha," I said to Sarah's belly. "It's time to leave Hotel Mama and join the rat race. I know it's hard to leave such luxurious accommodations, but there are good things out here, too. We're nice people, believe me."

"Just bring me another pillow," Sarah said.

We waited for four more days. Sarah went to work, came home, lay down on the sofa. I think each of those extra days felt like it lasted a month. Sarah had started to feel cramping.

"Is it a contraction?" I asked.

"How should *I* know?" she said. "I've never had a contraction before."

It wasn't to be. The twinges inside her stopped, and we didn't get to take our much-anticipated ride to the hospital. She learned that contractions were supposed to feel like menstrual cramps, but with a defined beginning and end. Finally she started to feel real, genuine contractions—but they were irregular and weren't going anywhere.

Sarah, always resourceful, had heard secondhand about a doctor recommending castor oil as a distinctly medieval home remedy for inducing contractions and coaxing reluctant babies out of the womb. We didn't have any evidence that it worked, but Sarah was willing to give it a shot. We bought a bottle and placed it on the kitchen counter. We stood there for a while, eyeing it warily.

"Isn't that stuff supposed to make you throw up?" I asked. I could tell by Sarah's expression that she didn't care if it made her grow an extra head, as long as it worked. "Never mind," I said.

She downed a tablespoonful.

"Feel anything?" I asked.

"I don't know." She put a hand on her belly. "Natasha, it's time to come out. Mommy says so."

"That's good," I said. "Appeal to her as an authority figure."

Maybe it was Mommy's edict, maybe it was the castor oil. Maybe it was just time. *Something* worked. Within hours Sarah started having real contractions. They weren't strong, and they were far apart, but she knew it was the real thing.

"I'll start shredding pots of water and boiling the sheets," I offered.

"Very funny," she said. "Look, it's going to be a long time

yet. You're making me nervous. Why don't you go play golf or something."

Play golf? I had just taken up the game that summer. I was terrible at it, but I liked it. Though it was December 4, the temperatures were supposed to reach the mid-forties that afternoon. In Minnesota, that kind of balmy day comes along only every twenty years or so.

"What about . . . um, the *baby?*" I asked.

"The contractions are so far apart that it's going to be a long time before we have to do anything," Sarah replied. "Just be back in an hour and a half."

Turns out Sarah had been reading baby books. She knew that first labors tended to be long, and hers was moving at a glacial pace.

"Play golf," I said. "OK, why not. Just don't have the baby until I get back."

I drove out to the par-three course by the airport. I had to wear gloves, and I shivered in the morning dew, but I played well by my standards. I pumped my fist as I sank a putt to par a hole.

Then I hit a traffic jam coming home, and my cool completely dissolved. *Great, I'm stuck in traffic and the baby's going to be born early and I'm not going to be there because I played golf and I'm already a failure as a father and what was I thinking and Sarah's going to give birth in a taxicab and . . . wait a minute, the traffic's easing up.*

I got home fifteen minutes later. I composed myself, went inside, and found Sarah messing around in the kitchen.

"Are we still having a baby?" I asked her.

"I think so," she told me. Her contractions had basically stalled out. She was still experiencing them, but they weren't growing stronger or more frequent.

In most cases, early labor is a waiting game. For most normal pregnancies, the hospital won't want to see you until the contractions are five minutes apart. Some women launch right into heavy labor, but it's more likely that you'll have at least several hours to kill.

Make the most of your time. Call your folks and tell them they're about to become grandparents. Do the dishes. Don't sit around staring at a stopwatch to time contractions—you'll just make your partner nervous. Double-check your overnight bag. Do some deep-breathing exercises. Congratulations, Dad, you're almost there.

By late afternoon we were in business again. Natasha was getting ready to join the outside world. The contractions were regular and about fifteen minutes apart, much less frequent than the magic five-minute interval that would mean it was time to go to the hospital, but officially heralding the beginning of labor. By nightfall we were getting tired of waiting. We were in luck, though. Our friends Teddie and Chris were throwing a party at their apartment a few blocks from our house.

"Should we go?" I asked.

"Anything to get a little distraction." Sarah sighed.

If you have the opportunity to go to a party while your partner is in labor, take advantage of it. Sarah was treated like a movie star, and I basked in her glory. The apartment was jammed with people, and a ripple of suspense spread through the place when word got out.

I could see what people were thinking. *She's in labor, for God's sake. What's she doing here? She'd better not start having that baby or I'm out the door.*

We went home around eleven. I went to bed in the guest room. A couple of hours later Sarah woke me up.

"The contractions are seven minutes apart," she told me as I rubbed my eyes. "And they're getting stronger."

I popped out of bed.

ANOTHER WAY LIFE ISN'T LIKE TV

Y ou probably learned about labor the same way I did—from watching TV. I thought that women grabbed their bellies and fell down, and that their menfolk then had to make a mad, freaked-out dash to the hospital. Hopefully a humorous episode might occur along the way—a parade blocking the way or a fender bender with a carful of clowns. Then a blustery cop would arrive, turn on his siren, and accompany the frantic couple to the hospital at full speed, brakes squealing and tires burning.

Here's a secret:

IT DOESN'T REALLY HAPPEN THAT WAY.

W e've all heard about one-hour labors, about children being born in the hospital parking lot. It happens, but rarely. Be prepared for a rush to the hospital, but keep in mind that you'll probably have plenty of time to get there. Even if you get caught in the St. Patrick's Day Parade, you'll make it. And if you don't, at least you'll have an interesting newspaper clipping to give your child when he's of age.

THE HOSPITAL—"I'M GOING IN!"

S o maybe you *wanted* to come screaming up to the emergency entrance with your engine smoking, like a subplot in *ER*. Believe me, it's better to be calm. Park in the visitors' lot, tuck your parking stub under the sun visor, and take your partner's arm to lead her inside. Her contractions are five minutes apart now, and they're starting to hurt. Be sympathetic, stay cool, and don't rush her.

You brought your overnight bag, right? *Of course* you did. And you had the foresight to pack it in advance. Think about tossing in the following stuff:

- **a change of clothes** for you and your partner. Remember that she's going to be significantly smaller around the middle than when she went in, but that her prepregnancy clothes still aren't going to fit. Make sure she has something comfortable to wear for the ride home. Also bring something for you to sleep in, and a nightgown for your partner in case she decides to shed her hospital wear.
- **an outfit for your child,** something in newborn size and appropriate to the season. The child will probably be smaller than you're thinking if you've never held a newborn, so don't pack the jeans and sweater in eighteen-month size.
- **food to eat.** You'll be in the hospital for at least forty-eight hours, and you won't want to subsist on hospital food alone—in my case, they didn't even offer to feed me. Bring dried fruit, crackers, juice boxes. You might not have access to a refrigerator, so forget the frozen pizza.
- **something to read.** At some point you'll find yourself sitting around doing nothing. You'll thank yourself for bringing something to read in place of venereal-disease pamphlets.
- **photos, stuffed animals, a boom box, and some music,** anything that helps create a comforting atmosphere for your partner during delivery and recovery afterward.
- **your car keys and some cash,** because you're going to forget something and have to run out and fetch it.
- **toothbrushes and toiletries.** Pack some travel-size samples in a bag and have them ready.

We brought along a big red rubber ball for Sarah to use during delivery—sitting on the ball affords the woman a comfortable perch during labor. We'd been warned that the hospital only had two big rubber balls, and that other mothers might arrive first and call dibs on them. I highly recommend this extra item, which Sarah found useful to sit on during the worst of her contractions.

MY DAUGHTER'S BIRTH

W hen you get to the hospital and the action begins, you'll be in a whole new world. If you're staying in the delivery room with your partner, scope out a good place to sit and start playing it by ear. Ask her if there's anything she needs. Keep breathing.

The story of each birth is as distinctive as the child that each birth produces. I offer you mine. I hope that you'll understand that, as varying as each experience might be, in the end we'll all become fathers. The universal thread that ties all fathers together is the emergence of our children into the world, and the monumental importance of that moment.

We arrived at the hospital at around two-thirty in the morning. We filled out paperwork, made our introductions to the midwife, and got accustomed to the atmosphere. The place was quiet, almost silent. We had our own room, and we closed the door. Natasha decided to take a final rest before being born, so Sarah and I napped for an hour until labor resumed.

I woke up in the dark hospital room. Sarah was talking to a nurse. I heard more activity than before, as the hospital geared up for sunrise. About fifteen minutes later we were transferred to the actual delivery room. It looked like a midline motel room, with a bed and a TV bolted to the wall. I had a hard time comprehending that this was where my daughter was going to be born.

After checking with Sarah, I broke the news to the midwife and nurse that I wasn't going to be in the delivery room during the birth. They looked surprised, and I felt a pang of guilt. I asked Sarah again if she wanted to change her mind. She said no. I told her that I was there if she needed me.

And then I left. I went down the hall to the waiting room, poured myself a cup of coffee. It was about five in the morning. Across the room was a Somali family; from their nail-bitten and exhausted look I could tell they'd been waiting for quite a while. The father was sitting with his two kids, and I imagined I could see him contemplating what it was going to be like to have another.

The coffee was terrible. I had no appetite. There was nothing for me to do, so I leaned back in my institutional chair and waited to become a father.

Brynnar showed up around six-thirty. He brought a thermos full of coffee and cigarettes for us to share.

"I figured you'd want these," he said, handing over the Marlboro Lights. "I know you quit, but . . ."

"You shouldn't have," I said, unwrapping the cellophane. "And look—you remembered my brand."

We took the elevator downstairs and smoked in the cool dewy morning. Hospital workers arrived in waves, sleepy-looking and steeling themselves for a long day.

"So how're you doing, buddy?" Brynnar asked.

He looked a little freaked out himself. I'd had him on notice for about three weeks. He had checked his messages every time he was away from his apartment for more than a few hours. Brynnar was neck-deep in an end-of-the-semester push, so I was grateful that he was willing to drag himself over to the hospital early on a Saturday morning to hold my hand—well, *metaphorically* hold my hand.

"I'm doing great," I told him, though I realized that my cigarette hand was shaking.

"Big old *Dad*," Brynnar said.

"That's me," I replied weakly.

We went back upstairs. I paced up and down the hall. Sarah's door was closed. I put my ear against it and heard muted voices. I waited there until a nurse came out.

"How's it going in there?" I asked.

"Fine," she said in a distant, professional manner. "You can go in anytime you like."

"I will later," I said. I didn't want to go in and interrupt Sarah's focus. The last time I'd seen her, the contractions were strong enough to make her wince. By now, I knew, they would be a lot more severe. I wanted to check on her, but we had an agreement. I knew that going into the room would accomplish little other than making me feel better.

The next couple of hours passed in a blur. Brynnar and I went downstairs again to smoke. My stomach was burning from nervousness.

"Are you hanging in there?" Brynnar asked me. He had an expression I'd seen before, one that said, *You don't look so good.*

"You bet. I'm doing great," I said.

When we went back upstairs I lasted about two minutes in the waiting room before I sprang up and went to the delivery room. I waited outside until a nurse emerged. I was painfully conscious of my absence from the birthing room, and vacillated between wishing I was there and feeling glad I wasn't. Part of me envied the man who chose with his partner to take part in the birth. It was a big decision either way, and now I was feeling the downside of the path I'd taken.

"Do you want to come in now?" she asked me.

"Can I?"

She laughed a little. "Of course. She's doing great."

Inside the room Sarah was perched on her big rubber ball. She was facing away from me. The room was very still save for the sound of her breathing, deep and regular.

"Is she . . . ?" I began. I sensed that I was intruding on a delicate moment.

"She's doing great," the nurse said again. "She's very brave."

I learned later that the nurse was in training to become a midwife. She would be a stalwart friend and supporter for Sarah throughout the labor and birth.

"How's it going?" I asked Sarah. A little voice yelled at me inside my head: *Stupid, stupid, stupid. How does it look like it's going?*

Sarah lowered her head as a contraction hit. She was off in her own world. I could tell that she was handling the pain well, and felt a swell of pride. I also got a glimpse of what it would have been like to have me in there the whole time, asking inane questions like *How's it going?*

The pain seemed to subside. Sarah looked up at me. Her hair was hanging in sweaty strands on her forehead and neck. Her hands balled into fists, then relaxed. She started to say something, and I could tell that it required a lot of effort to speak.

"It's *really hard*," she whispered.

Yikes!

I felt a rush of emotion: sympathy, empathetic pain, most of all a fruitless desire to make her feel better. The midwife came into the room, and I got a sense of how superfluous I was to the process.

"I'll be outside," I told the nurse. Then, pointlessly, I added, "Let me know if you need me."

The nurse nodded curtly. Sarah didn't respond; by then, she was deep in her own world again.

No one was thinking about me; no one was worried about me. This was how Sarah and I had planned it. This was the moment when I realized that I wouldn't ever feel guilty again about not having been in the delivery room. We had made the right decision—*for us.* Sarah didn't need me there going *pant pant pant, hee hee hee, pant pant pant.*

As I left, I looked back. A deep understanding came to me. Sarah, the midwife, and the nurses were deeply involved in something basic, almost primordial. This was *deep dark female stuff.* I could sense these women bonding, drawing strength from each other and becoming more than the sum of their parts. Later Sarah would tell me that the support and companionship of these women got her through the delivery.

I haunted the halls. This was taking a long time, longer than the timetable I'd carried in my head since birthing class. By then it was about nine-thirty in the morning—more than a full day since

Sarah had felt her first contractions and sent me off to play the Rich Acres golf course.

I leaned back against the wall and let my head drop to my chest. When I looked up again, I saw a group of fathers-to-be and their pregnant partners shuffling down the hallway. I suddenly realized that this was a childbirth-education class taking a get-acquainted tour of the maternity floor—the same tour I'd gone on months before. I was sweating and light-headed, and a few of the men in the group looked at me with fearful recognition.

I felt like a beggar in some Victorian novel: crazed, feverish, dressed in rags, and banging a tin cup on the ground.

Once I was like you, squire. Just like you.

The door to Sarah's room opened. A nurse came out. She looked serious; I searched her features for some sign of what was happening. She recognized me, composed herself, and tried to smile.

"She's doing all right," she said. "We can see the head. It won't be much longer."

More time went by. *Too much.* Nurses came and went. I had stopped going to the waiting room to check on Brynnar. I stood there in the hall alone, too tense to talk, feeling more helpless than ever before in my life.

Then I heard noises inside the room. I took a step closer to the door. At first I thought it was the baby crying. *The baby has been born, and no one came out to tell me.* I put my hand on the doorknob, ready to let myself in.

Then I heard another noise—a high-pitched cry. I heard a couple of women's voices offering encouragement.

I realized that it wasn't my daughter I had heard crying through the door. It was my wife. Sarah was inside that room crying out in pain, in a voice I had never heard before.

Holy shit.

I was plunged into a completely unfamiliar emotional universe. I don't remember what I did next. I might have paced some more, I might have just stood there. All I remember is the sound of those cries and the knowledge that Sarah was trying to push out Natasha's head so the little baby girl could be born. Words like *anxious* and *worried* are totally inadequate to describe what I felt. I was worried about staying on my feet. I feared something had gone wrong.

"You can do it," I heard the midwife say. Her voice was loud and distinct through the door.

"I can't," Sarah sobbed.

Oh, *man.*

I was glad I wasn't in there. I couldn't make that baby come out. I also knew that, even if I could have hidden it, I would have been *completely freaking out.* At the same time, this was the moment that I wished I could have been in there to somehow help.

A couple of minutes later the door opened. A nurse stuck her head out.

"You can come in now," she said.

"You mean—"

She nodded. I went into the room. The air was heavy, the lights dimmed. There seemed to be a lot of people in there, and they were doing things I didn't understand. A surgical screen was set up over Sarah, and the midwife was preparing to start stitching.

Sarah was holding our daughter. Sarah was dazed, exhausted, mildly traumatized after a long labor. She was beautiful.

I felt like there weren't enough tears to cry.

"You did it," I said to Sarah, stroking her hair. "I'm so proud of you."

"Our daughter," Sarah said. I looked down. Natasha's face was red, her eyes were closed. She was so small. I recognized her face from the ultrasound images. She had finally come out to live with us.

I hadn't thought much in advance about how this moment was going to feel. Mostly I had just hoped that everyone would survive, and I'd left it at that. But now it had happened. Natasha was alive and well. I was a father.

She was the most beautiful and amazing thing I'd ever seen. She was less than five minutes old—just like in the Stevie Wonder song—but already I loved her more than anything or anyone else in the world. I reached out for the rail on the bed to steady myself, suddenly realizing that I might pass out.

No matter what else ever happens to me, I know that this was the best moment of my life. Everything good in me, and everything worthwhile in this universe we try and fail to understand, touched me in that moment and I was forever changed.

Most of this book is about what you can do for your child. But you'll soon find out what your child will do for you. Your child will make your heart ache with love. She will make you *feel* more than you ever did before. Sometimes I think that Natasha gave me faith in myself, because she showed me how great my capacity for love is. I'll always be grateful to her for that.

MODERN MEDICINE STEPS IN

Before I even had a chance to hold my child, a nurse whisked her away and put her on a little tray under bright lights. I almost protested, but I realized I was in a delicate state and would probably sound like a lunatic if I said anything. Instead I took a step back and watched in dumb confusion as a pair of nurses started to poke and prod Natasha. They made notes on a chart, exchanged mumbled asides to each other. They sounded detached, a little skeptical. I started to think something might be wrong with the baby. My heart sank.

Be warned: they're going to do this to your child as well. *Don't worry about it.* The chances are very good that everything is fine. This is a routine check of your child's breathing and vital signs, along with the Apgar test that measures the newborn's reflexes and physical health. At the end of the test they assign each baby a score—don't lose your mind when you learn that your baby didn't rack up a perfect grade.

Newborn babies are pretty beat up. They've been squeezed through the birth canal only to find that they're no longer in the womb. It's hard for them. They have absolutely no idea what's going on. They might have marks on their bodies from the passage out of their mother, and sometimes they suffer from minor health problems that take a day or so to clear up.

Natasha had some fluid in her lungs, which the nurses efficiently took care of. Because she had baked in the oven a few extra days, her feet were dried out, scaly, and red. When the nurses were done with their exam I finally got to quiz them.

"Natasha's all right? She's all right, isn't she? I mean, she *looks* all right. That means a lot, doesn't it?"

The nurse smiled as though she'd heard this line of questioning more times than she could count.

"She's healthy," she told me. "She came through just fine."

Relief flooded me like a drug. I felt like dancing. I suddenly realized that I was still crying. I hadn't stopped since I'd taken my first look at Natasha.

Sarah was paying no attention. She seemed not to even notice that she was no longer holding the baby. She winced with discomfort as the stitches were applied and the midwife pushed out the placenta. Sarah looked as though she had been through a long, hard battle.

Which, after all, she had.

Brynnar came in and met the baby. Pretty soon he was on his way, back to his own life after this strange interlude. Finally the nurses gave Natasha back to her mother. Sarah and I looked at her for a long time, crying and laughing at the baby's feeble gestures as she tried to move her body after being pressed into the womb for nine months.

An orderly came to transfer Sarah to the room where we would spend the next forty-eight hours. I accompanied a nurse down to a room where newborns are given their first bath. Natasha went in and out of consciousness, cried and complained, took a magnificent shit, and basically endured her first bathing experience. I snapped pictures and checked out the other two babies in there with us.

It was unbelievable. These little babies, squinting and frowning, belching and pissing, were brand new to the world. Each one was like a universe full of possible futures and new sparks of brilliance and love. I wanted to point at Natasha, to say *This one is mine. And I'm hers. Can you believe it?*

When it was time to go, the nurse sort of prodded me toward the door. I obeyed. It turned out that I was going to do a lot of obeying in the next couple of days.

Because I was going to be a guest of the Maternity Marriott.

6

The Maternity Marriott

The Hospital Stay and the First Days
After Going Home

Your partner has endured labor and childbirth, and you've both had the privilege of meeting your newborn daughter or son. The birth, however smooth or however traumatic, will have been something that took place in a sort of altered reality for both of you. There's really nothing to compare it with, and it's a difficult experience to place in the context of everyday life. But soon reality returns.

About an hour after the birth of your child, the enormity of what just happened sets in. The adrenaline wears off, and you realize that you're emotionally and physically drained. You need to lie down in a comfortable bed, close your eyes, and zone out for a while.

Well, *good luck*. The Maternity Marriott is many things, but it will not seem like a restful sanctuary—at least until you realize you have to go home and live without all the little amenities you took for granted.

THE MATERNITY MARRIOTT

You're booked for a two-day stay at the hospital. If you're lucky, maybe you've never stayed overnight at a hospital before. The operative concept is *boredom*. Imagine the worst hotel you've ever stayed at. At least the Roadside Inn on the interstate has a swimming pool. The Maternity Marriott features tiny cans of apple juice and a TV with a remote control that may have been designed in Romania during the last days of the Ceauşescu regime.

Our room featured a big adjustable hospital bed for Sarah. She settled in, exhausted. I looked around. Where was *I* supposed to lie down? The answer loomed in the corner: a little chair upholstered in burlap. A nurse came in, pulled off the cushion, and unfolded it into an incredibly narrow sort of Hide-A-Bed.

"That's *it*?" I asked.

"Make yourself at home," she told me. "We call this 'The Rack.' "

This bed, this cot, this . . . I don't know what to call it, but it was so narrow that my elbows hung off the side when I lay down. It creaked ominously when I settled in. The metal joints of its frame poked through the thin mattress and pressed against my body's vital nerve centers.

"That doesn't look comfortable," Sarah said, her eyes heavy with fatigue.

"There's a reason for that," I replied.

Natasha was asleep in her mother's arms. I turned on the TV. Soap operas and talk shows were all I could find. There wasn't even an episode of *Judge Judy*.

"What are these channels?" I asked. "I don't think we even get these channels at home."

It was like a parallel universe. There were similarities to other hotels I'd stayed at: the room was either too hot or too cold, the plastic cups came wrapped in cellophane, and working the telephone required a doctorate from CalTech. But there were differences as well. Nurses came in without knocking to inspect Sarah and the baby. There was a panic button in case something terrible happened. And there was no mint on the pillow. In my case, a mint might have hidden the pillow from sight and made it impossible to find.

"Do you think we should call up people to come visit?" Sarah asked.

"I don't know about that," I said. "I'm not sure I want anyone to see me like this."

A word of advice: In the aftermath of your baby's birth, either you or your partner might be completely exhausted. After you've made your phone calls to parents and close friends, you might need to chill out in relative peace for a while. Think twice about making commitments to entertain a lot of visitors at the hospital—especially the first day. Wait and see how the three of you feel before inviting anyone over. Sarah and I ended up having only one visitor during our two-day stay in the hospital, which was really all we felt we could handle at the time.

Our friend Teddie visited us for a while, holding Natasha and making us feel connected to the outside world. Time began to drag. The baby slept nearly all the time, and there was really not much to do. I drove home to feed our cats, feeling as though I was on parole.

That night we were awakened by the baby's crying. She gurgled and complained from her little bassinet. Sarah and I sat up, my spine giving a nice little pop as I disengaged myself from The Rack.

"The baby's crying," I said.

Sarah got up and held Natasha. The baby still cried. She didn't want to eat, she didn't want to sleep. She just wanted to cry. It was two in the morning.

"How does this work?" I asked.

And then it hit us: *we had a baby.* I didn't know anything about babies. I didn't know what to do. Luckily a nurse came in and took Natasha to a nursery down the hall so we could sleep for a couple of hours.

The next morning a nurse burst into the room, looking scared and businesslike in the same moment. We were watching TV while the baby slept.

"What's the matter?" the nurse asked us.

"What do you mean?" I asked.

"You pushed the panic button. Is the baby all right?"

Sarah looked around on the bed. She pulled out a plastic contraption. "Is this the panic button?" she asked. "I was lying on it."

I started to adapt to my surroundings, like a convict serving a sentence. I learned that, if I asked nicely, I could cajole extra juice boxes from the food-service lady after she'd stopped at all the rooms. I didn't really want more juice, it was just something to do.

"You know something?" I said to Sarah as the idea dawned on me. "When we go home, there won't be any nurses to help us out with the baby. It'll just be us."

We stared at each other in horror.

A typical hospital stay after an average birth with few or no complications is two days. The stay will be longer after a cesarean section, a surgical procedure that involves an anesthetic. After a C-section, a new mother can expect to remain in the hospital for about three or four days if her recovery progresses normally.

COMING HOME/ALL PRESENT AND ACCOUNTED FOR

You filled out the forms for your daughter to get a Social Security number. You dressed her in that little outfit you packed about two months ago. You stashed away all the pilfered diapers, shampoo, and cotton swabs that you can carry from your hospital room. It's time to check out, and take the baby home for the first time.

As it turns out, you might not want to leave. This is a variation of the *Helsinki Syndrome,* in which hostages come to sympathize with their captors. The nurses who were such a pain in the ass at first have become your best friends. They take the baby away when you need to sleep, they bring you little cartons of apple juice when you're thirsty. Suddenly you realize that none of them are coming home with you. Your two-day stay in the Maternity Marriott is over.

"I won't complain anymore," I promised. "Just don't make me go home."

A nurse will come downstairs with you to make sure your infant car seat is the right kind and that it's been properly installed. Aren't you glad you already put it in the backseat and checked to make sure you did it right? Now you can load up your newborn child, say good-bye to the nurses, and go home.

As you're driving home, you experience a creeping sensation. This is the first time you and your partner have ever been truly alone with the baby. Ominously, the baby will be in a rear-facing seat and you won't be able to see her. You fight off the irrational fear that she's back there suffocating—don't worry, she isn't. This will also be the moment when you remember that:

• you never fixed that cracked window in the living room—the one that will let in a draft and make your child catch pneumonia.
• you have absolutely no idea in the world how to change a diaper.

• you really should have given this whole thing more thought before you got into it.

• you're uncertain of the torque/impact ratio impacting your baby's body when you drop her—although you're certain you *will* drop her, probably in the next couple of hours.

• your life has suddenly become extremely scary.

You glance over at your partner and smile, your hands on the wheel, the master of the road. The very picture of the new young father. It's imperative at this point that you don't admit that *you're completely unprepared and have absolutely no idea what to do*. Your partner has just given birth, and she's dealing with her own sense of uncertainty. You might be scared to death, but physically you're all right—so consider yourself responsible for setting a calm, confident tone.

In fact, your partner is probably doing much better than you. Chances are, she's fantasized about having a baby her entire life. There are some things she's not sure about, but she knows that essentially everything will take care of itself.

As for the baby, she's exhausted from the rigors of being born. Her senses are raw and unformed. She doesn't know *what* she is, much less who she is and what's going on. It will be a couple of weeks before she even has the energy to let out a good, earsplitting wail. She needs a warm place to sleep, a breast to suck on, and arms to hold her.

Turns out you're the one with the problem. Unlike your partner, you don't have a river of hormones surging inside you, helping you feel your place in the cosmic scheme of things. You've spent the better part of your adulthood putting fatherhood on the same level as, say, a prison sentence or conscripted military service. You got yourself in the right frame of mind, you kept in mind everything good and great about being a father, you were truly looking forward to it. And suddenly you realize you're about as suitable for being a father as you'd be to pilot the space shuttle.

Take a deep breath. Keep your hands on the wheel. Don't let that smile turn into a grimace.

You're certainly right to be afraid. You probably *don't* know what you're doing. This is when you need to remember a guiding principle:

IT'S GOING TO BE HARD, BUT ANYONE CAN DO IT.

i f necessary, chant this to yourself a few times like a mantra.

There's no way to be qualified in advance for what you're about to undertake. It's all on-the-job-training. You might make a mistake or two, but everyone will survive. The next week or so is going to be difficult, but you'll come through it. Relax; don't worry too much. You want to do the right thing, and that's the main prerequisite for the job.

Now, steel yourself for the new paradigm of your existence: a finely wrought combination of chaos and sleeplessness.

BABY TIME: STRANGER THAN FICTION

B y now you've probably entertained a number of images in your mind about what fatherhood is going to be like. Chatting with a friend in a cafe about the philosophical implications of artificial intelligence while your blessed offspring quietly draws abstract landscapes next to you. Walking through the park on a windy day, your natty tweed blazer buttoned up, explaining to your daughter why the sky is blue and how birds are different from airplanes. Standing in an open-air market, your arm muscles rippling fetchingly as you carry your child while picking out fresh produce.

It's not going to be like that at all, not for a while at least.

The first month of taking care of your child can be summed up in one word: *maintenance.* You're the first-day technician on a Rube Goldberg contraption, doing five things at once like a frazzled character in a silent movie.

If you can, take a leave from work. Use up your vacation time if you have to. Your partner is going to need help in these early days, while she's still recovering from childbirth. If it's impossible for you to take time off work, at least understand why your partner is so burnt-out and frazzled when you get home at night.

Taking care of a newborn is a lot of work, it's not always rewarding, and you're going to be exhausted all the time. The good news is that things are going to get better very soon. Your beautiful child is going to develop a personality, start to crawl, and eventually come to think you're the funniest, strongest, greatest dad who ever walked the planet.

Until then, you're going to learn a new way of looking at time. Night is day, day is night. You're going to learn whether your child is hungry, sleepy, bored, or in need of a diaper change. She's going to start training you through regimentation, the sending of subtle signals, and, when all else fails, the Piercing Wail.

You used to sleep seven or eight hours, get up, work, play, work out at the gym, spend some time with your spouse or your friends, have a drink, go to bed, then get up and do it all over again. Those days are gone for now. You are living in Baby Time, a parallel universe in which pacing the floor at three in the morning is as perfectly natural as a deep slumber at three in the afternoon.

You need to learn to go with the flow. The good news is that, for the first couple of weeks, your baby is going to sleep almost all the time. Remember, childbirth is very traumatic for the newborn. Imagine if you were pressed through a two-foot-wide tunnel for eight hours, inch by inch. You'd probably be ready for a rest when you were finished, and so will your baby. She'll sleep nearly all the time.

Unfortunately, her metabolism won't be geared up for the eight-hour blocks of sleep that we thrive on—and won't be for quite a while. She'll sleep a couple of hours and wake up, crying for food. She'll totally amaze you by sleeping four hours at a stretch, although tomorrow at the same time she'll go down for fifteen minutes and wake up again.

She will be unpredictable. As soon as you think you see a pattern in her sleep schedule, it will disappear just as quickly.

This brings us to our next guiding principle:

LEARN AS MUCH AS YOU CAN ABOUT YOUR BABY, BUT NOTHING IS ETCHED IN STONE. AS SOON AS YOU LEARN SOMETHING, THINGS WILL CHANGE AND YOUR KNOWLEDGE WILL BE USELESS.

Maybe you aren't that adept at going with the flow. Maybe you consider yourself a control freak, someone who likes to regiment his life. You might have certain expectations of the world and those around you, a sense that they should conform to a rational order of things that you consider healthy and sane. If that's the case, you're in deeper waters than you can even imagine.

It's a very Zen concept: You get a grip by letting go. Let go of your sleep schedule. If you're awake with the baby at three in the morning, don't think about how tired you're going to be tomorrow. If you're alone with the baby and talking on the phone when she wakes up crying, tell the person on the line that you have to go. If you need to change a diaper in the middle of dinner, remember that you can always reheat your food if it gets cold.

So let's say you take this to heart. You make your best effort to remain fluid and unflappable. You drag yourself through the day when you're about to weep from sleep deprivation. You learn to hear your baby's crying as a beautiful sound in its own way, her only means of communicating her needs in this strange new world in which she finds herself.

But you're still going nuts. Why?

Because you're *human*. The fact is, a newborn baby is an irrational animal. She has no identity, and little personality. She doesn't understand her own needs, her senses are unformed and primitive, and she experiences life mostly as discomfort, and will until she's a few more weeks old.

Here's something to remember: Caring for your baby might seem like an infinite, daunting challenge right now, but before long she's going to be walking around and starting to talk.

You're going to think how fast it went, and you're going to be amazed that the days of infancy are gone.

You're also going to remember how hard it was, hopefully, and pat yourself on the back for getting through it.

But it's already slipping by you. Someday soon your daughter won't be a baby any more. Keep that in mind when you're changing a diaper at three in the morning, or enduring a crying fit while you're trying to drive on a crowded freeway. Try to enjoy the little things, and give yourself warm memories to look back on when it's over and she's moved on to the next stage. Because at some point your eyes are going to mist up, and you're going to hear yourself spouting the cliché: *she's grown up so fast.*

The first week of infancy is enough to drive you nuts. But be strong. This is an honest-to-God, real-life *trial,* a test of your mettle. Wouldn't you like to be remembered as someone who took it well, who was always graceful and together, who was an admirable young dad? Of course you would. Who wouldn't?

And take it from me: pretty soon she's going to start smiling and laughing. Your happiness will totally hinge upon her goofy grin—and she'll do her part to keep you going.

It will be great. Every day it'll get a little better. Trust me.

SLEEP DEPRIVATION: ADVENTURES IN EXHAUSTION

I t's important to know in advance that sleep deprivation is going to be your prevailing reality for the next couple of months. I like sleep the way a gourmand likes food. If some is good, then more is better. Nine hours a night tops me off nicely.

Forget about it. The first couple of months of Natasha's life, I never slept for more than three or four hours at a stretch. When I did sleep, it was in a bizarre state of readiness. The newborn child is in pretty much a state of constant need. And, after Mom, you're the one who can fill those needs.

The good news is, you might have some interesting hallucinations.

I drove to the supermarket with a list clenched in my hand, wondering whether my shocks were in really good shape or if my car really was floating a few feet above the road. I had gone to bed the night before at 10, then got up at 11:30 because the baby was crying. I went downstairs with her, rocked her, went back to bed at 12:30. I slept until about 2, when the baby woke up crying and hungry. Sarah fed her, and I went back to sleep. I woke up once again, I'm not sure when. I may have gone downstairs for a glass of orange juice, or else I dreamed it. Then we all got up at 6, the baby's natural waking time.

Was I tired? Probably so, although I couldn't be certain about much of anything. My eyes felt funny; my food tasted strange. I stared at an article in the newspaper until I gave up trying to make sense of it. I had been tired before, but this was different. I had pulled all-nighters in college, but I usually crashed the next night to compensate. This was serious, long-term, unrelenting sleep deprivation. I tried to remember if I'd signed up for a sleep-clinic experiment and forgotten about it.

I learned to enjoy the feeling, frankly. The supermarket was really nice: loads of colors, soothing music playing. Soup in a cardboard carton—now what genius thought of such an innovation? I wandered around, picking up most of the things on the list, wondering why people were looking at me funny.

I now know: They were looking at me strangely because I was shuffling around with a glazed expression on my face, taking an inordinate interest in the gaudily hued labels on canned chili. I had turned into an automaton, waking and sleeping blending for me into a not-altogether-unpleasant fugue state.

Then I got out to the parking lot. The first thing I realized was that I'd left the groceries inside, that I would have to go back and embarrass myself by asking for the stuff I'd paid for and left behind. I gently leaned my head on the steering wheel.

Who was I fooling? This wasn't pleasant at all. I couldn't think straight. Everyday errands were beyond my capacity. Working was almost impossible. Soon I would lose my job and go broke, my meager savings consumed by baby clothes and gaily colored, overpriced things purchased to placate my daughter. I was going to have to live on the street with my family. I would turn into one of those guys who compose poems on the spot for a little pocket change. My life was over.

Get a grip, some inner voice said to me. *Things will get better. One day you will sleep again.*

The inner voice was right. Things were going to get better. But not for a little while yet.

When I got home I took a rattle out of the voluminous box of gifts Natasha had received before she was even born. I sat down on the carpet with her and waved it in front of her eyes. She didn't even notice it. Nobody had told me that babies can't even play until weeks after they're born.

THINGS YOUR BABY CAN AND CAN'T DO

You might never have been around a newborn baby before. If you have, you handed it back to its mother as soon as you sensed you were in over your head—say, after about thirty seconds.

Your newborn is very small, very weak, and having a hard time adjusting to the reality of being an air-breathing human being after an idyllic nine months spent in the womb. You, on the other hand, are ready to go. You want to start playing with the mini–basketball hoop and ball you bought last month. Hold off for a little while.

When your baby is one to two weeks old, she can:

- **maintain brief periods of semialertness,** in which she will gradually start to notice that you're there.
- **notice lights and sounds** (sometimes). She sees blurred shapes and a little color. Try a book of big, black-and-white pictures to start stimulating her vision and interest in the outside world.
- **begin to recognize voices**—including yours.
- **sleep, eat, shit, cry.**

Your baby *can't:*

- **do much of anything** besides just lie there. Even basic motor function is a few weeks off, so toys are basically useless.
- **smile**—not until about three or four weeks at best. For now, if she smiles, she's probably having gas pains.
- **differentiate between faces.** But convince yourself otherwise. It'll be more rewarding.
- **sit, roll over, or hold her head up** on her own. Don't get any big ideas about teaching her to crawl when she's a week old. The muscles just aren't there yet. Try folding yourself into a warm sack and not moving for nine months, and see how athletic *you* are.

LET MY PEOPLE GO

We both know that a big part of a man's identity is his freedom. There's the freedom to be who he is, to think what he thinks. There's also the freedom to come and go as we please, to hang out with whomever we want whenever we want. As for the former, you'll always have the freedom to be who you want. But as for the latter, you can pretty much kiss *that* good-bye for a while.

I think that every man has an ideal in his head of a perfect day. It probably starts with getting up at around ten or eleven in the morning, knocking off a stack of pancakes with bacon, climbing a hill in the sun, playing some basketball, and maybe hunting deer with a crossbow, followed by an evening with friends in a "gentleman's club" downing shots of bourbon from between a stripper's cleavage.

And then you'd like to get up the next morning and do it all again.

Fathers of babies don't get to do these things, at least not all day. For one thing, your sleep patterns are going to be shot for a few months. You're going to be tired and cranky. You can still go play golf or ride your bike, but you have to plan these activities more in advance and take it like a good sport when circumstances conspire to keep you at home. You'll probably want to cut down on the skydiving and ax-throwing—can't have you dying on us now. And as for the strippers and the booze, well, that's between you and your partner. Be understanding if she's lost her sense of humor about such nocturnal endeavors.

It isn't going to be easy. We want to do as we please, when we please. But your baby is going to have a completely different agenda from yours, and she's going to have a lot of needs. It's going to be your job to make sure these needs are met.

You're going to experience a fairly dramatic drop-off in your personal freedom, my friend, at least for now. Take it like a man.

You'll be repaid with respect. Who needs a grumbling, recalci-trant, bickering father and spouse? Your partner doesn't—she's already going to have *one* child in the house.

Having a baby changes things dramatically, and not always for the better. But here's some deep wisdom about small children that will serve you well, both in anticipating the baby's arrival and in living with her after she's born:

IT'S GOING TO GET MUCH, MUCH BETTER. AND SOON.

emember that this is *your life,* and you're only going to live it once. There are no rehearsals, and there's no going back to cor-rect our mistakes. We should all want to live our life well. And when you're a new father, this is going to mean subordinating your own needs in favor of the child's. Derive satisfaction from a job well done—and keep in mind how good it will make you feel to be able to look back on early fatherhood and *know* you did it right, with strength and patience.

Being a father means being a man. And a man doesn't com-plain because he would rather be out playing with his friends than helping his partner care for their baby. And a man doesn't bear grudges in his heart because having a family has kept him from doing whatever he wanted at any given time.

Now, get ready for the big change. And remember that no one's perfect.

7

When Two Become Three

Your Relationship With Your Partner During and After Pregnancy

OK, guys. I know you're tempted to skip over this chapter. But your partner won't—in fact, this might be the only one she's going to read. For most guys the words *let's talk about our relationship* are about as comforting to hear as *we'd better take a sample and send it to the lab*. But talk about it we must, because during pregnancy and after the birth of your child you and your partner are going to face unique challenges in romance, sex, and keeping your relationship healthy and rewarding.

The important thing to understand is that things are going to change. Hopefully you figured this one out already. The question is: How are things going to change, and what can you do to help make sure it's a change you can both live with?

THIS IS NOTHING LIKE WHEN
WE WERE DATING

t he physical changes a woman experiences in pregnancy take hold quite a while before her belly begins to grow. Hormonal shifts, different moods, changes in sleep patterns, and nausea and fatigue will become major elements of your partner's daily reality. Already the baby has become a presence in your lives. Somehow it no longer seems like the world is composed of just the two of you, even though the baby's birth might yet be months away.

You've given thought to what kind of father you want to be, and you've tried to be considerate of your partner's needs. But a big question is looming, one that you might have a hard time putting into words. Let me help. The question is: *What kind of relationship am I going to have in the future with my spouse?*

You start to realize how easy you had it in the past. You had tons of free time to spend together: you were still blissfully unaware of each other's annoying habits. But now it's getting harder. Sometimes you start to worry about what kind of life you're going to spend with each other. You wonder if the dream of family life you might have enjoyed is going to turn into a strained and difficult reality.

Well, my friend, this is adulthood. And it's not easy. But it's not as though you have no control over your reactions and your attitudes—and this is an important fact to fall back upon and remember when the sky darkens and the seas turn stormy.

Your relationship with your partner is going to change. It's changed already. Acknowledging this fact now will save you difficulty and disappointment, and will help you to view clearly where your life together is going and what you want it to be.

You're going to have much less time for just the two of you. On the whole you're going to have less fun for now—at least fun as you might currently define it. You're both going to be under new pressures and demands, and either of you at any given time might not be at your best. And you're no longer going to be the central focus of your partner's life.

It sounds worse than it is. Honestly. Each relationship between two people is different, but if there's a connection of trust and respect between them everything else will fall into place—as long as both parties keep from pushing the panic button when times change.

Observe the changes. Effect the changes. Try to get the most out of the changes. But don't fight and decry the changes. Just because your partner is paying less attention to you doesn't mean she doesn't love you anymore. And imagine how she'll feel if she's forced to deal with your complaining about her actions and attitudes at the very moment when she's trying to deal with her impending motherhood.

You're going to be a dad. That means you have to be a man, and not a boy anymore. A boy expects to be coddled and catered to; he expects the people in his life to put his interests first. A man knows better, and lives accordingly.

It's hard for men not to be selfish. And believe me, we *will* be selfish, no matter how hard we try. But we can temper our self-interest with compassion and reason. We can start to put our family's interests ahead of our own. And we can give our partner a break. She doesn't need the added pressure of our disappointment and disillusionment over our realization that life isn't set up to gratify our adolescent desires. She needs a partner, a father for her child, a man.

BUT MEN STILL GET TO HAVE SEX, RIGHT?

Is there sex after pregnancy?

I should hope so.

And there's no reason why you can't have sex *throughout* the pregnancy. I wouldn't do it on a roller coaster, but pretty much everything else is fair game. As the pregnancy progresses and her belly gets bigger—not to mention her overall level of discomfort—you'll find that some sexual positions become difficult or impossible. Use your imagination; if you're both eager and willing, you'll find a way to make it work.

Pregnant women are beautiful; there really is such a thing as a pregnancy *glow* that women give off. Make sure you convey throughout your partner's pregnancy, and after she's given birth, that you still find her attractive. Small gestures go a long way: a kiss, a compliment, a little clandestine hand-holding when you're out in public.

Each woman experiences her pregnancy differently. Some pregnant women are completely turned off to sex, while others are more interested than ever. It should go without saying that you'll need to be understanding if your partner isn't as eager as usual to have sex with you when she's pregnant. She might be tired, it might have been a long day, she just might not feel like it. Don't make her feel as though she has to explain herself.

In the early days of a romance, sex is an expression of mutual attraction and lust. In a long-term relationship it's more tricky. Hopefully the attraction never goes away, but the act of sex becomes a more nuanced expression of intimacy and closeness. Recognize that trying to maintain the connection between the two of you during pregnancy and beyond is now the name of the game. Focusing on your needs exclusively can damage that connection and hurt your sex life in the long run.

I *know* this is frightening stuff. But it doesn't have to be. If your partner isn't interested in having sex with you at the moment, remember that she will be interested another day. As long as she feels all right about saying no now, she'll feel all right about saying yes later.

The lessons you've learned about the changes in your life from becoming a father will also serve you well in dealing with your partner. Stay flexible; stay calm. Keep an eye on the big picture. Remember that things won't be this way forever.

NOW EXACTLY HOW IS THIS SUPPOSED TO WORK?

And then your partner gives birth. You're dropped right into probably the biggest challenge of your life: dealing with your newborn infant. You feel stressed, you never get enough sleep, you're *just getting by* a lot of the time.

Still, you'd like to have a little sex once in a while. But how? When? There isn't time, there isn't a place. . . . This is not how you thought things were going to be. *My God*, what have you done?

All right, time for a deep breath.

First, the days after your partner gives birth will not be a sexual wonderland. Many women experience injuries related to childbirth that preclude sexual intercourse for a given period of time. Her doctor will tell her when it's safe again. Sex can also be painful for a woman in the weeks after childbirth, and she might have to become comfortable with her body again. It's not uncommon for her to need time to work through an association of sex with discomfort, and to become relaxed enough to feel pleasure from being with you.

Be supportive and compassionate. This does not have to be a crisis in your relationship. It's natural and understandable. Remember that you can kiss and touch without engaging in headboard-rocking activity. This is a good time for you to take pleasure in little intimacies with your partner. And here's a little secret you might have lost sight of: Sexual intimacy between two people is based on the mutual world they create and share. A tender touch, a kiss, or a kind word help create an atmosphere in which sexual expression becomes more of a possibility. Take these first days after childbirth as an opportunity to get in touch with your closeness with your partner.

Frankly, this is harder than it sounds. You might think that a little making out on the sofa is a great idea, while your partner might not want to be touched at all. Don't be offended. Remember that her body is adjusting to no longer being pregnant, and that her moods might fluctuate. She's dealing with the pressures of the new baby alongside these physical changes, and it'll take time before she feels completely like herself again. If you're loving and supportive, she'll have an easier time readjusting and getting in touch with her sexuality.

OK, this hasn't been easy, but we can both stop squirming now. Let's talk logistics.

MY LOVE DEN HAS BECOME A PLAYPEN

Even if you and your partner are both interested in sex at a given moment after your baby is born, you've only halfway reached your goal. First of all, the baby is always around. Who knew? It's like she's *moved in* or something. On any given Saturday afternoon the baby might only be comfortable napping with her mother or with you, giving you no time alone. And she's too young to slip ten bucks and send to the movies.

You're going to have to look at the situation constructively and do your best. If the baby will only nap with you today and not in her crib, then that's that. Don't get angry or frustrated. You'll have your day.

Essentially you're down to three segments of time in which you have any possibility of enjoying sexual activity: nap time, after the baby goes to bed for the night, and when the baby is out of the house.

Nap time is optimal. The baby is asleep—you have a little taste of freedom. If you can stay awake long enough you might get to enjoy yourself. This is a very good reason to encourage crib naps.

After the baby goes to bed for the night is also a good moment, although the baby might be sleeping in bed with you for a while. Take heart. Soon she'll be old enough to sleep in her crib. Eventually she'll even sleep through the night—although don't hold your breath waiting for it to happen. In any case, you'll have blocks of time in which to catch up on your reading, make phone calls, clean the kitchen, and engage in carnal activity.

When the baby's out of the house is best. You're not worrying about the baby; you don't have one ear trained to the monitor listening to the baby's gurgles and coos. A trusted baby-sitter and a plan can do wonders for Mom and Dad's relationship.

You have a problem, however, if the baby's crib is in your bedroom—which it very well might be, depending on how much space you have. Your love nest has been invaded by a little creature. The answer, of course, is to have sex someplace else. Put the baby down for a nap and proceed accordingly. Go to the living room, the kitchen, wherever. That's not so bad, is it?

Make the best of your time and try not to focus on how much easier things used to be. The past is gone. Reviving your sexual relationship with your partner might take time, it might take planning, and it might take more effort than it used to. Sometimes you might both be interested but it simply *isn't going to happen,* because the baby needs attention. It isn't going to be a simple matter. But really, isn't it worth it?

PASSING ON THE MANTLE OF KING BABY

Once there's three of you instead of two, nothing will ever be the same again. Get used to it, and you can make it work.

And get into it. Enjoy the moment. Don't cloud your mind

thinking about how things used to be, or how you think things should be. This is your life—live it well.

The last thing your partner needs is to have two babies at the same time. I'm talking about her having to deal with both your infant and with you acting like one because you aren't getting your way. Men can send nasty little signals to their partners once they have children: *you used to be fun, you used to think I was sexy, you used to be more interested in me.*

She still loves you. And she'll love you more if you step up and act like a responsible, sane, and considerate partner and father.

Each man harbors a little tyrant inside him. I call him King Baby. King Baby wants to be adored and gratified. King Baby demands attention and validation all the time. King Baby wants other people to make him feel good about himself. He wants his ego stroked. He wants to feel important. King Baby wants a lot of things, and if he doesn't get them he's going to make his displeasure felt. If he's not happy, then *no one* is going to be happy.

How do I know this? Because I'm a male. King Baby lives and breathes inside my heart. King Baby wants to know why his life isn't arranged to give him more fun, more pleasure, more attention.

I simply have to let King Baby have his say, then proceed with my life with as much maturity and strength as I can find in the better parts of my character. King Baby isn't going away. But King Baby doesn't have to rule.

If you conduct yourself like a man, then the world will approach you like one. Treat your partner with respect and affection, and try never to lose sight of why you wanted to be with her. She's the mother of your child, which is a place of unique honor in your life. Be patient, be strong, and your life with your child and with your partner will improve. Trust me.

8

Brave New World

Life With Your Baby After the First Week

After the first days with your newborn, a thin ghost of a routine might have started to form. It's probably a routine composed of sleeplessness, chaos, and confusion, but you'll take what you can get at this point. The baby starts to seem like less of a space alien and more like your child. You start to realize: hey, this isn't going to be easy, but I think I can pull it off.

You're alone with your son, for the first time. Your partner is in the shower, or taking a well-deserved nap. You're holding the sleeping baby when he suddenly wakes up and starts to cry. This is it. It's happening. You have total responsibility for this beloved little creature. Resist the urge to clomp upstairs and hand him over to your partner. This is your moment to be a real Daddy.

WHAT I'VE LEARNED

t aking care of a newborn is truly a form of on-the-job training, and what follows is based on my own experience. This is all information you will eventually figure out, but here are a few guidelines to help you through the early stages of your baby's life.

When a newborn baby cries, one of four things is wrong with him:

1. He's sleepy. Well, he was sleeping in your arms for a couple of hours before he woke up, so we can rule that one out in this case.

2. He's hungry. This is a good possibility. If you're breast-feeding exclusively, maybe you *do* need to wake up your partner. But why not try a bottle? If Mom has pumped some milk in advance, have some ready, warming in a pan of warm water. If you're using formula, you're already in business. Hold the baby in one arm while you get the bottle together. Administer. If you're lucky, the crying will stop.

Sometimes it's not so easy. My daughter took a bottle without complaint a couple of times when she was about a week old. Suddenly, during my third time feeding her, her eyes opened wide. She looked at me, then at the bottle poised over her face. A single, overwhelming thought went through her mind: *I'm being cheated! This isn't Mama!* She began to wail uncontrollably, a situation that got even worse when I offered her the bottle again. We'll talk soon about bottle refusal and how you might be able to deal with it.

3. He needs a diaper change. This is another culprit. Think about it. If you moved your bowels in your underwear, then sat in a drafty room for fifteen minutes, you'd be ready for a little freshening up, too.

If you don't know how to deal with diapers, this is your golden moment. Open diaper. Clean up mess with diaper wipe. Put on new diaper. Have someone show you the first time. It's like riding a bike—after the first time it's a snap. And pretty soon you'll wonder how you ever got disgusted by anything.

🐌 **4. No reason that you can discern.** You're not in the Fussy Period yet; with luck, maybe you never will be. But remember, the baby's senses are developing every day. He's taking in new, unfamiliar stimuli, like the sight of your unshaven, bleary-eyed face staring at him in uncomprehending frustration. No wonder he's crying, come to think of it.

Some new parents experience a syndrome in which Mom's way of doing things becomes the norm, and when Dad tries to get involved he feels as though he's inept or inadequate. First of all, you're not inadequate. But if you don't get involved with taking care of your baby, you're always going to be behind your partner's learning curve. Ways of dealing with an infant are learned through hard-won experience, and if your partner is locked into certain ways of doing things it's probably because of the struggle she went through in order to develop her own techniques. Talk it out. Listen to her. Get involved and pretty soon you'll be able to give *her* advice.

And don't worry about being clumsy and hurting the baby. Babies are sturdy, and you'll be careful. And although every other baby you've ever held felt fragile and delicate, you'll find that your own baby doesn't. Why? Because you're getting to know him, you're feeling comfortable with him, and you're developing confidence that you're the guy to care for him. Now *that's* a good feeling.

And here are a few more handy concepts:

• **Gas.** Babies have a lot of problems with gas. They fart a lot, and belch like longshoremen. The period after a feeding is particularly perilous. You have to feel sympathy for them; their digestive tracts are still developing, and their inner workings have yet to hit their stride. Imagine bad gas pains coming every few hours, all day, every day. You'll start to get a picture of what reality is like for the baby.

If you fed the baby and he starts crying, he's probably having gas. He needs to be burped. Rest his chest on your hand and lean him forward slightly. Pat him on the back with your other hand until he belches. Or until he throws up all over your hand. One or the other will probably bring him some relief.

• **Diaper rash.** This is very easy to recognize: red, irritated skin around the genitalia. You might not be changing that diaper often enough, partner. As you well know, that's sensitive skin down there. Pain there is enough to make anyone cry. Put some over-the-counter medicine on it and it'll clear up in a day or so.

• **Discomfort.** Remember, your child is a miniature human. If he seems irritated, maybe his clothes are too tight. Maybe you put his diaper on backward. He might be too hot, or too cold. Maybe he wants to lie or sit in another position. Think on your feet and keep trying.

TV, YOUR NEW BEST FRIEND

T V is a depressing cultural wasteland. Bland, insipid sitcoms. Implausible police dramas. Insulting newsmagazines. Endless sports highlight shows. Oh, those sweet endless sports highlight shows.

Whatever your feelings about TV, you need to realize that it is now a valuable resource for you. You're spending a lot of time tending your baby, and you need a form of distraction that leaves your hands free to deal with him. You're burnt-out and exhausted. Sometimes your baby needs to sleep in your arms for hours at a stretch. That new translation of Dante you've had on the shelf for a few years has somehow lost its appeal.

Face it: it's time to reexamine your opinion of Don Johnson's acting abilities.

The first couple of months of my daughter's life, I gave in completely to television. I rocked in the rocking chair, my sleeping child in my arms, and watched *SportsCenter.* And CNN. *Homicide: Life on the Street. Talk Soup.* Christopher Walken on *Inside the Actors Studio.* VH1's *Behind the Music.*

And here's the great thing: I was taking care of my daughter, being a good father, taking the strain off my wife—yet at the same time I was learning about the torment and downfall of Milli Vanilli, and the intricacies of the New York Giants' latest quarterback controversy. I was getting credit for being a great guy and a responsible father, but in reality I was indulging in total mind rot without feeling a shred of guilt about it.

Don't tell anyone you heard it from me. Just make sure you get cable before the baby's born.

There are going to be times when you feel as though you can't take it any more—the lack of sleep, the boredom, the stress. Don't worry: every parent feels this way sometimes. Start finding little ways to make the hard times bearable, if not enjoyable.

The baby's crying and won't stop. It's the middle of the night and you need to sleep. He won't eat, he won't sleep. He doesn't know what he wants and, if anything, his crying is getting more intense. You're alone. You feel like you're losing your mind. Suddenly your frustration takes over, and you feel like you're losing control. You get an urge to shake the baby, to make him stop screaming for just a second.

Don't do it.

According to one study, injuries from shaking account for one in ten infant deaths from abuse and neglect. Symptoms from shaking injuries might not even be apparent at first, but violent shaking can easily produce debilitating brain damage.

According to a 1995 study, 70 percent of those who shake babies are men.

Please remember that one shaking episode can permanently disable or kill your child. Know this in advance, before the rage sets in and you lose yourself for a second. I remember one night at about two in the morning when Natasha wouldn't stop crying. I felt the impulse to shake her, and it scared the shit out of me. I put her down on the sofa, wrapped her in a blanket, and took a few steps away while I composed myself.

Remember that there are times when taking care of a baby is overwhelming. It's OK to feel that way, and it's hard for everyone. Put the baby down, call someone if you have to. Take deep breaths. Remember how much you love the baby, and how you would feel if anything bad ever happened to him. A single rash moment can undo everything you care about.

FIVE TIPS FOR STAYING SANE

1. Every baby book gives the same advice for parents with newborn children: *sleep when your baby does.*

Which is no problem, as long as you can adjust to sleeping about ninety minutes at a time, during apparently random shifts throughout the day and night. Nonetheless, they're basically right. When your son goes down to take a nap at six P.M., crash out on the sofa until he wakes you up again. Forget about the dirty dishes for a day. Don't worry about returning phone calls. Look at yourself, man—you need to sleep. Take it when you can get it.

2. If you're like me, you might have scaled back on your ridiculously self-abusive coffee consumption during your middle to late twenties. The stuff makes you jittery; it's hell on your stomach. It's bad for you.

It's time to get cozy with the coffeepot again. I went from a cup a day to six or seven in the first weeks of my daughter's life.

Now I'm down to about four. Sure, caffeine is a crutch. And, right now, you're going to *need* a crutch or two.

3. Even newborns respond to music. Not hard-core hip-hop or avant-garde jazz, typically, but they do enjoy less challenging offerings. My daughter seemed to like high-pitched, gentle music. I put a boom box in her room and, when she went to sleep, I popped in one of a few lullaby tapes I bought for just this purpose. They're familiar to her, and the music helps her get to sleep. I've also tried ambient atmospheric tapes of rain falling and gentle breezes—the kind you heard in New Age bookstores and prided yourself on never owning. A word of warning about the lullabies: they have very touching lyrics that you will interpret as tales written expressly about your sweet, beloved, defenseless little child. Go ahead, sit on the bed and weep. It'll make you feel better.

I have two words for you: bouncy seats. You can find them in the baby section at the department store. They're essentially hammocks that enable the baby to rest in a semisitting position. Often they come with a little battery-operated vibrating box that comforts and soothes the child.

The bouncy seat is fantastic in the early days because it enables you to put your child down someplace without leaving him sprawled on the floor or the couch. It comes with a little seat belt that holds the child in place. Now you're free to pour a cup of coffee or to curl up in a fetal position on the floor.

We had an extra bouncy seat, and when our friends Gary and Julie were expecting, I pressed the extra seat on Gary.

"Take it," I said. "You'll love it."

He looked at it uncertainly. It was hideous, a multicolored contraption of cloth and metal.

"OK," he said. "Thanks."

After their son Henry was born, I was on the phone with Gary. "Hey, thanks again for that bouncy seat. Henry loves it."

"Ahh . . . the bouncy seat," I said knowingly.

All kids love the bouncy seat. And every parent comes to love it too. It's hard to explain until you've been there. Having the baby resting happily on his own is somehow the greatest thing in the world. You begin to learn how much pleasure you can derive from the smallest of things.

4. At some time around three weeks of age, many babies enter into what is known as the *fussy phase*. Your tranquil, sleep-all-day angel is probably going to start crying—loudly and, it might seem, all the time.

The fussy phase is the dirty little secret of parenting. Many parents don't even want to admit that their baby is fussy, because the fussy phase can be intense and unpleasant for the unprepared. A lot of negativity can begin to tinge the air when an infant cries and cries and won't stop, and it's often an experience that can really shake up a parent.

Forewarned is forearmed, my friend.

You will know fussy crying because of its difference from regular, I've-just-moved-my-bowels-in-my-pants crying. Fussy crying is *rhythmic and intense*. Typically the baby closes his eyes tight and will kick and flay at the air with his fists. Essentially, it's a storm of newborn rage, and it can be pretty unsettling the first time you have to contend with it.

Here's the deal with the fussy phase. Throughout the day the newborn becomes increasingly hard to please and agitated. By dinnertime his sleep and waking cycles are getting shorter and shorter. Then, at around eight or so, the baby loses it. He cries and cries and won't stop. You try everything, and you and your partner start to feel exasperated. You feel like a failure. And you don't want to admit how irritating it all can be.

The fussy phase is nearly universal. There's no consensus on what purpose it serves, if any. By twelve weeks of age, your baby is going to grow out of it. In the meantime, the name of the game is coping.

First of all, realize that your baby has to fuss. Make sure his diaper is clean, that he's eaten, and that he's comfortable. After that, realize that there's only so much you can do. A fussy baby spirals out of control, and often too many attempts at placation seem to irritate the baby even more—and, as a result, a half hour of fussing can be transformed into a three-hour odyssey.

My best advice is to split up. Send your partner to bed while you deal with the baby, or vice versa. There's no reason both of you should have to endure the noise and tension. Realize that the baby is going through a brief phase, that you've done nothing wrong, and that there's nothing wrong with the baby. Try rocking, singing, holding. If the baby is in a rage of rhythmic crying, put him down in a warm safe place—and make sure he can't roll and fall. (Even on a sofa, a raging baby is capable of flipping himself over.) Let the baby cry for three minutes, then five, then seven. Alternate these periods of crying with two minutes of holding. Eventually the baby will tire himself out, and you'll be spared the experience of having him scream in your face nonstop for an hour.

It's not easy to put down a crying baby. But after a baby has cried himself out, he'll be calmer and more restful during the night. If you can learn to recognize the fussy phase, and have a plan for dealing with it, I guarantee you'll save yourself hardship and heartache.

And if you're among the minority of parents whose babies don't really fuss, thank the fates. Oh, and don't tell the rest of us—at least until our babies are finished fussing.

There is a sort of innate, preverbal communicative quality to the sound of "shh." If you make this sound gently and quietly to even a newborn child, he seems to understand somehow that you're trying to calm him. It's the power of "shh," and a lot of the time it actually works when a baby is in the emotional zone between crying and being receptive to consolation. This will turn one day, though, when the baby realizes you're trying to get him to shut up and, like any self-respecting person, gets mad at you and yells even louder.

🐦 **5.** The best tip of all is to hold your child up and look into his eyes. He's causing you some grief, but you know he can't help it. He's starting to recognize you and love you. And your heart is starting to melt as well. The kid's two A.M. crying doesn't seem that bad after all, not after he's smiled at you for the first time or started to make gurgling sounds of pleasure at the sight of your face.

The whole story of the newborn is a complex one. There's a lot more frustration and difficulty in the package than many parents are willing to admit—for one thing, you start to forget after it's over and to gloss over any past unpleasantnesses. This is healthy in the long run. What you'll probably most remember is the first time you sat alone with your son in a quiet room in the middle of the day, the sun streaking through the windows, and cried tears of joy over his very existence. That's what it's all about. Now come on, get ahold of yourself. There's more you need to know.

THE NEW REALITY: YOU DON'T MATTER AS MUCH AS YOU THINK

Y our child will naturally gravitate toward your spouse. The child knows his mother is where the action is, be it food, reassurance, or basic safety. It's biological, totally hard-wired into his conception of reality. In the days to come you'll develop a good relationship with your child—at least, you'd better—but you're also going to feel a bit superfluous at times.

It doesn't help that your partner isn't paying as much attention to you as she used to. You used to be a mysterious, intriguing sex machine. Now you're the guy who got her into this mess. She might be stressed, might snap at you. She'll hand you the child without even looking at your face.

You might want to ask "Hey, what am I? Nothing but an extra set of hands and an occasional paycheck to keep the kid in diapers?"

A tip: *Don't ask that question.* You really don't want to hear the answer.

All of a sudden it's going to dawn on you: If you're like most guys, you used to be the child of the house. You drank too much sometimes and made an ass of yourself. You indulged in whacked-out hobbies and let yourself get into splendid emotional funks that lasted weeks at a time. All of it added to the wonder that was you.

A warning: It isn't that amusing anymore. Every minute you stay out past your professed coming-home time is a minute your spouse has to deal with the kid alone. Every time you indulge in sophomoric depression over the senselessness of the world and the stupidity of society is another instance your partner has to use up precious energy dealing with you—if she's even still inclined to pull you out of your postadolescent morass.

Some new mothers experience postpartum depression, the so-called "baby blues." It's easy to understand why your partner's emotions might be a little out of whack. Her hormones are changing as her body regains equilibrium after pregnancy. She's been through a very intense experience (childbirth), and she might feel the repercussions only after a little time has passed. And she's been through so many changes in the past year that it might all be overwhelming. Some women even report missing being pregnant, when their child was inside them and was theirs alone.

Like anything else, this will change and should get better. The best way to be supportive is to help out with the baby and offer kind words. If she seems down, encourage her to talk about what's going on. In some extreme cases the "baby blues" indicate clinical depression, with strong feelings of anxiety, sadness, and hopelessness. If you think this is happening with your partner, sit down with her and get her feelings out in the open. Clinical depression is serious business, and seeking professional help is not only a good idea for some new mothers (and fathers), but a sign of willingness to ensure that the new family is healthy and strong.

It's time to be a man, my friend. Put in the extra effort; do the right thing. You really have no choice—not if you want to be a good father and partner. Look at it this way—you had many years in which society and your partner indulged you. You got to play around in college, and you probably spent some time afterward figuring out who you were and what you wanted.

Who you are is a *father*. What you should want is to be a *good* one. Don't worry, you're still you. You have your dreams and your eccentricities. It won't be long before you can pull them out again, give them a test run to see if they're still charming. For now, though, you're no longer the child of the family. Handle it with grace. Someday you can exact your revenge by visiting the kid at college, getting drunk, and embarrassing him in front of his friends by regaling them with the story of how he used to pretend to be a puppy.

I HAVE NO FRIENDS

It starts to happen right away. When Natasha was about a week old, my friend Juan in Boston called. We talked on the phone a few times a week, our conversations inevitably drifting off into metaphysics and speculative philosophy. We both loved it, because we had each found someone else who wanted to talk about UFOs, noir movies, and NBA basketball for hours at a time.

Now, though, the tone had started to change.

"Hey, man," Juan said. "How's that kid?"

"Great, great," I replied. I looked at my watch. Juan had called about five minutes after Natasha went down for a nap. Already I was calculating lost time I could have spent drooling in a semicatatonic state on the sofa.

"Is she healthy and everything?" he asked.

"Yeah, healthy like a horse. Someday she's going to play in the WNBA. Just you wait."

Silence. I sat down heavily on the couch. I sensed myself getting antisocial, regarding contact with my family and friends as an intrusion on my precious catnaps.

"Man, I can't believe you have a daughter," Juan said. "It's too much. I mean, doesn't it blow your mind?"

"Yeah," I agreed. "It does."

"Anyway," he continued, "I was reading this thing on James Joyce in the *Times Literary Supplement*. Did you see it?"

"No."

"It was really contentious. I don't think it was fair," Juan said, getting animated. "I'm thinking about writing a reply."

The TV was playing without sound in my living room. Hockey highlights. I don't care about hockey. Still, it looked interesting—things moving around, pretty colors. I snapped back into reality.

"You should see a little child eat," I said, apropos of nothing. "You start to think about little things. I mean, today she ate, what, her thirtieth meal of her life or something? Isn't that incredible?"

"I guess so," he replied.

"And I got this little chair she can sit in," I went on, oblivious to his uninterested tone. "It operates on batteries, and it vibrates. She really likes it."

"I see," he said.

I then complained about my lack of sleep, the complexities of my daughter's bowel movements, my mixed feelings about taking her outside during the arctic Minnesota winter. After a few minutes of this, I sensed I was losing my audience.

"Well, anyway," I said. "You get all wrapped up in this stuff."

"Hey, I understand," said Juan. "It's great."

"Yeah, it's great."

"Really great."

"Yeah, incredible."

"Really something."

"A big-time head trip."

I heard my own voice—flat and toneless. And it was then that I remembered talking to Ross months before. I sounded just like he had: burnt-out and exhausted. I had come full circle.

Juan went back to his girlfriend and his doctoral thesis. I went upstairs and checked to make sure there were enough diapers. Our interests were diverging fast.

I had essentially the same conversation with other friends over the course of the next week. They were into their lives, their work, dealing with their girlfriends or spouses, or else their energy was spent trying to acquire girlfriends and potential spouses. They were going out to movies, going out for dinner, staying up late. Suddenly I couldn't relate to any of it.

The fact is, your life has changed. You have a child, and your consciousness is permanently altered. This is a *good* thing. The problem is, you're going to feel like you don't have any friends anymore. In your darkest moments, you're going to look out on the barren plain of a future in which the phone never rings and the only people you associate with have children—and want to talk exclusively about nothing but their offspring's cute comments and stunning aptitude on the piano.

It doesn't have to be like this, not if you don't want it to. For the time being, your friends might leave you alone out of respect and consideration for the demands now being placed upon you. You're tired, stressed; you're putting all your energy into your spouse and child. Your good friends will realize this. In a couple of months you can start to reestablish your bonds with the people you care about. If they're up for it, they'll see that your life has different priorities and adjust accordingly. If not, they'll probably slip away. But this is what happens to adults. Part of being a man is recognizing it, accepting it, and moving on. Besides, they're probably just jealous.

9

The Days of Milk and Diapers

The First Few Months With Your Newborn:
Problem-Solving, Spending Time
Together, and How Barney Can Make
You a Better Father

The first few months of the baby's life are easy for a
father, in a sense. It might not feel that way, but compare your plight with that of your partner. The newborn infant has eyes only for her mother. Her
relationship to your partner is her most basic and primal reality, and will be until the baby is able to discern
and recognize you. It's great when this happens, but
with privilege comes responsibility.

Your daughter's first act of branching out in the
world will be forging a relationship with you. Welcome her with open arms, talk to her, sing to her—
above all, make her understand that you *want* to be
with her. Babies pick up a lot of nonverbal clues, and
I tend to think they understand a lot more than we
might assume at first. Get in the game and start
spending time with your child. The more you do, the

more you'll want—that's how it works. The better you know the baby, the better you'll be able to read her subtle clues and preverbal signals. And the better you and your baby will get to know each other—after all, you're going to be around each other for a long time to come.

A FATHER TAKES CARE OF HIS CHILDREN

A lot of new fathers don't take this basic concept to heart. They think—openly or secretly—that taking care of the child is the mother's job. They look upon dealing with their kids as a chore. They talk about *baby-sitting* their children. Listen:

A FATHER NEVER BABY-SITS HIS OWN CHILDREN.

Some time ago, I clipped an article from *Redbook* magazine, called "Dad's Fair Share," that offered strategies for women trying to get their partners to spend time with their children.

Frankly, this is *pathetic*. Consider the mind-set of a woman who has to try to coax her partner to take care of their kids. This woman lives in a world where the children are her responsibility, and the man has to be manipulated into *helping out*, or *baby-sitting*. Think about it. Is this the kind of family you want to create?

SPENDING THE DAY

I spend every weekday alone with my daughter. You might not. Maybe you work from nine to five and then take care of your child in the evening. Perhaps you'll find yourself caring for your child only on the weekends, for a few hours at a time. Whatever the case, new fathers fear spending blocks of uninterrupted, one-on-one time with their babies. We don't know what to do, or what babies want. The only remedy is to jump in and improvise.

The first time I was alone with Natasha, I was *terrified*. For the first month and a half with Natasha, Sarah was always around. I had taken care of Natasha on my own, but Sarah was always somewhere in the house.

Natasha was about six weeks old; I was thirty. I had an advantage in size, intellect, and worldly experience. Nonetheless, I knew that she had the trump card of a temperamental meltdown, which she would drop on the table the moment *anything* started to go wrong.

Sarah decided she wanted to go to the gym, which was innocent enough. Forty-five minutes or so on cardio machines, maybe lift some light weights. She didn't even shower at the gym, preferring to wait until she got home. So the whole thing would take, at most, an hour.

"Super," I said. "Haven't I been saying that you need to get out, to do something for yourself, make some space for yourself? It's about time."

Translation: Go if you must. Leave me here for everything to degenerate into a state of horrible ruin. Be a bad mother. Fine.

OK, I could handle this. Natasha was fed, and I held her in my arms as Sarah went out the front door, gym bag in hand. I watched from the window as Sarah's car backed out of the driveway, then disappeared around the corner.

I looked at Natasha, who was staring into the middle distance, lost in the complexities of baby consciousness.

"This'll go just fine," I told her. "As long as we understand each other. I have no milk for you. I'm sorry, but that's the way it is. You don't like to drink from the bottle, so you're stuck for an hour. Maybe if you were old enough to play on your own, color in a coloring book, something like that . . ."

I trailed off. Natasha's eyes were widening. She sensed a disturbance in the force. She made a little half-strangled sound of wary apprehension.

"Who needs coloring books?" I asked her in my best placating voice. "Let's sit in the rocking chair. You like that."

She looked around, her head unsteady on her developing neck muscles. *Where's Mama?*

What would keep *me* happy in this situation? A book, a magazine, a long-distance phone call . . . no good; none of them applied. Natasha gurgled, I sensed her bottomless baby anger beginning to boil up to the surface.

Then I saw it. The baby swing. In my mind's eye it might as well have been bathed in a golden nimbus; it was a gift to me from some benevolent mythological pagan god, a means of satisfying the primal monster that threatened to engulf my little village in tears.

I carefully put her in it, making sure not to smack her head against what I called the "bonkin' bar," a slat of light metal built in the perfect location for striking the infant forehead.

Natasha grunted, coughed. She looked around. I buckled the belt, cranked up the device, put a blanket on her lap, sent her swinging.

I sat down to watch her. I felt completely exhausted. Sarah had been gone less than five minutes, according to the clock that I glanced at every thirty seconds or so. Fear was making my heart beat double time. If this didn't work, I didn't know what I was going to do.

An image appeared in my mind: a tableau of me pacing the floor, carrying a red-faced, screaming Natasha over my shoulder. With every turn on the rug, I would look at the clock, counting off the minutes while Sarah chugged along on the stationary bike.

The swing made its metronome sound. *Creak-a. Creak-a. Creak-a. Creak-a.* Natasha looked up at me, then let her eyes sort of droop a little. She was leaning back, her head resting against the swing seat cushion.

Creak-a. Creak-a. Creak-a.

My God. It was working. She closed her eyes, then opened them quickly, as though surprised to realize how fatigued she was, how close to drifting off. A few more back-and-forths, and her eyes closed. Within thirty seconds she was snoring.

I flipped on the TV and found a basketball game. Natasha slept for an entire hour in the swing. The only action required of me was that I get up every five minutes or so and recrank the thing. When I saw Sarah pulling into the driveway, I got the baby out of the swing. The two of us met Mama at the door.

"How did it go?" Sarah asked warily. "I was worried about the two of you being alone for so long."

"Worried?" I asked. "Whatever for?"

"Well, it was the first time," she replied.

I shrugged, a gesture that said *Balderdash. The king of all fathers can be left alone with his baby daughter for an hour. Maybe even two.*

"Would you please take her?" I finally said, handing the baby over. "I need to go lie down for a few minutes."

I started to spend more and more time watching TV while I was taking care of newborn Natasha. We'd rock in the rocking chair, and she'd fall sleep while I zoned out. Maybe it was just me, but it seemed as though everywhere I looked there were terrible fathers as the focal point of movies. I started to catalog them in my mind, thinking of all the ways that I might mess up being a dad. On the other hand, I couldn't possibly be as bad as some of these guys.

Bad Movie Dad Hall of Fame

1. The Great Santini

In this film, Robert Duvall plays a military father distinguished in his household for his unpredictability and the harshness of his iron-fist style of fathering. Also, he browbeats his son while playing hoops in the driveway. Truly cringe-inspiring to imagine myself turning out like this.

2. At Close Range

Christopher Walken plays a homicidal dad just released from prison who tries to reassert his authority over the rural gang he once led. He sports a bad mustache, plays his two sons' emotions with sociopathic expertise, eventually knocks off one son to keep him quiet. I didn't see much danger of my turning into this creep, but by a certain point in the film I couldn't be entirely sure. My self-image was taking a beating.

3. The Empire Strikes Back

Darth Vader seems to have abandoned his children. He becomes the Lord of Darkness. And he slices off his son's hand during a battle to the death. It's scary to think of yourself in about twenty-five years, breathing heavily, dressed in black, saying *I'm your father.*

4. King Lear

In this filming of a 1980s stage production starring Laurence Olivier, Lear alienates the only daughter who's looking out for his best interests, while surrounding himself with flatterers and rip-off artists. This bodes ill for our AARP-eligible years.

5. Night of the Hunter

Robert Mitchum is an evil preacher bent on killing his stepchildren. He has *Love* and *Hate* tattooed on his knuckles. A very scary take on the nontraditional family.

Which bring us to the all-time great movie for fatherhood role models: *To Kill a Mockingbird*. Gregory Peck plays a small-town attorney who defends a black man who would otherwise be dealt harsh Southern injustice. He's moral, upright, and great to his kids. Watch this one if you're ever feeling down on fatherhood.

WE ALL HAVE TO EAT

There are plenty of schools of thought on the topic of breast-feeding and the gradual weaning of a baby. I was blissfully unaware of all of them until Natasha was three months old and Sarah's maternity leave abruptly ended—until then, Sarah had simply breast-fed Natasha whenever the baby cried for food. But at three months I had to get involved.

Here's what the issue of breast milk boils down to: Breast milk is basically better for a baby, especially a newborn. Manufactured formula (a chemically engineered milk substitute) is second best—which is not the same as saying that it isn't good. *Of course* it's good. Read the label on the formula box and you'll feel fine about giving it to your child. Just look at all the nutrition that they cram into it. You'll be tempted to have a glass yourself (don't; it tastes bad). Modern science is just fine with me. I was raised on formula.

Some women don't breast-feed at all after they leave the hospital. There are plenty of reasons for this: It's not possible, or not feasible because of the demands their work places upon them. Some women don't breast-feed because they don't like it. This is not a sin; it's a matter of *choice* that no one should be made to feel bad about either way. Others insist on breast-feeding the baby until it's a year old, or even older.

You might have feelings about this matter, but the ultimate decision isn't really up to you. Unless you miraculously grow breasts.

It's best to give your baby a good start on life by breast-feeding her as long as possible. Extended breast-feeding in the first year of life has been linked to all kinds of health benefits. Another advantage is that, if mother and child catch the same virus, the breast milk will contain antibodies to the virus and the baby won't get as sick.

But this isn't a moral issue. There's no reason to feel bad about raising your baby on formula. For many mothers, breast-feeding is never convenient. If you have to put the baby on formula early on, the last thing you should do is harbor doubts, somehow feel like a failure and a bad father. Your baby will be fine. As long as she's getting adequate nutrition and a loving home environment, she is a lucky child with terrific parents.

We were fortunate enough to have the circumstances and material resources for Sarah to breast-feed our daughter for quite a while. Natasha drank breast milk almost exclusively until she was about three months old, when we started mixing in formula. It sounds so *easy*. But it was hell—a complete breakdown of my relationship with Natasha. It was a time of deep dark Trouble.

THE INCOMPREHENSIBLE HORROR
OF BOTTLE REFUSAL

After three months, Sarah went back to work. She carried with her an electric breast pump, an insane contraption that involves placing clear plastic cups over a woman's breasts while a little motor wheezes and moans. Somehow the mother's milk is then deposited into little plastic bottles, which Sarah would dutifully bring home for me to feed to Natasha the next day.

The Trouble didn't happen overnight. Like all good Trouble, it had first appeared a couple of weeks before and nagged at us, shaded our consciousness with anxiety. At first there was no Trouble at all. When Natasha was about three weeks old I fed her a meal from the bottle—electrically pumped breast milk, next best thing to the tit. Fantastic.

"Hey, I can feed her now," I said with ridiculous naiveté. "You can pump milk and then go do stuff, leave her with me. This is going to open up a lot of freedom for you."

Silly man.

I figured the problem was solved. But it was about two full weeks before I tried bottle-feeding Natasha again. Throughout Sarah's maternity leave, my best intentions about fostering her freedom from the baby didn't come to much. Sarah wanted to be with Natasha, and I wasn't very eager to be completely on my own with her.

"You should try to feed Natasha again," Sarah suggested. "I'm going back to work in about a month."

"You think I should?" I asked, looking up from my newspaper. A voice inside cried out: *a month? "*All right. *If you say so.*"

If I hadn't known better, I would have thought she was worried or something. I picked up Natasha, took the bottle, and showed it to her. She regarded it with utter indifference. I put the rubber nipple between her lips. She closed her eyes and began to suck. So far so good. I plopped down on the sofa, Natasha cradled in my arms.

About thirty seconds later she stopped sucking. Her eyes opened. She looked up at me, then the bottle, then back at me again. I could see the web of alarm developing in her mind. She pushed the nipple out from between her lips. She started to wail.

"Don't cry," I purred. "Here, eat. You'll feel better."

I tried to put the nipple back in her mouth, which made her cries of anguish turn to howls of anger and frustration. She started to writhe in my arms. Her face turned deep red.

Boy, these little babies have a remarkable capacity for anger.

Sarah was watching from the doorway. "Here, give her to me," she said. A real nipple was produced. Natasha was instantly quieted, happy, eating her lunch with gusto. *Well, that was interesting,* I thought.

Of course, the next time was even worse. Natasha seemed to remember the previous episode. She slid even more quickly into a state of paroxysmal baby rage. We tried again and again, varying the circumstances—having me feed the baby alone in the bedroom, with Sarah downstairs, having Sarah leave the house altogether, even having Sarah herself try to feed Natasha the bottle. The baby was having none of it. She absolutely would not drink from a bottle. Czarina Natasha had laid down the law.

This was called *bottle refusal,* logically enough. If your baby takes formula from bottles early on, you won't have to deal with this. But chances are that at some point you're going to come up against a stubborn and recalcitrant infant. Natasha was not going to budge on the bottle and, sure enough, the time soon came for Sarah to go back to work. Sarah was going to be gone for about ten hours a day. The only way Natasha was going to get any food during that period of time was to take a bottle.

Obviously the baby was going to starve to death. Three months in, and it was over already. I remembered all the houseplants I'd killed during my single days, and shuddered.

I was alone with Natasha. Sarah was at the office. She'd topped off our three-month-old before leaving that morning, giving Natasha the gift of a full belly. Natasha moaned and writhed in her bouncy seat while I read the paper, then took a nap on my shoulder. So far so good.

But then it was about ten-thirty—no, I thought with growing anxiety, closer to eleven. Natasha hadn't eaten in about four hours. I pulled out one of the bottles of breast milk, put it in a pan with hot water from the tap. Soon it was warmed and ready. Natasha looked up at me. She knew it was time to eat. Somewhere in her primitive little brain a question was forming: *Where is the tit? Food means tit. I am hungry.* The first stirrings of dismay began to form in her eyes.

I filled the bottle and took Natasha upstairs, figuring I would feed her in bed, her favorite place to dine with Sarah. I plopped her down on her side, lay down next to her, and slid the nipple between her lips.

She was crying before the nipple even got there. Tears streamed out of her eyes. She started gasping for air, crying louder and louder with a deep *desperation* that immediately infected me.

"Hey, fine, no problem," I stuttered. I picked her up, rocked her. She sniffled and quaked. She *had* to be hungry. I took her downstairs, put some of the milk into a little cup, propped the baby up in her bouncy seat. Natasha looked at me with curiosity as I raised the cup to her lips and poured some milk in her mouth. A lot came right back out—she didn't know how to drink yet, of course. She started to choke on it, but some of it was going in; I was sure of it. Finally she turned her head and started to cry. I picked her up.

This wasn't going so well. When Sarah got home that night the baby drank lustily from her mother's breast, her relief and hunger evident from the gasps she emitted between sucks.

"How much did she eat today?" Sarah asked.

"You don't want to know," I said.

It got worse the next day. I started to get obsessive. Each bottle of breast milk contained four ounces. Sarah was pumping two bottles a day. I figured two or three ounces at a meal was a good amount of nutrition. So far I wasn't sure if I'd gotten Natasha to ingest even a single ounce.

"You have to eat," I said to my uncomprehending infant. "Come on. *Please.* It'll make you feel good, honest."

She looked up at me and started sucking the air. *Tit, please. Now.*

The second day started to really bring me down. Natasha ate very little, taking a perfunctory suck on the bottle before dissolving into tears of rage. She drank a few swallows out of a cup, choking, crying.

By the third day I was ready to lose it. My every instinct told me to protect this baby, to make her healthy and whole, to keep her from harm. But goddammit, she wouldn't *eat*. I held her, talked to her in a soothing voice. Each time I tried to feed her, she would open her mouth and wail, turning red. She sounded as if she were being injured.

Then I got an idea. Not a good idea, but an idea. I did something that I'm even now not particularly proud of.

I knew that the bottle would shoot out a little stream of milk, like a squirt gun, if I pressed on the bottom of the plastic liner. Natasha was propped up on the bed, her mouth wide open, howling with anger.

So I did it. I pressed on the bottom of the bottle and shot a stream of milk right into her maw. Her eyes opened: she stopped crying for a second as she tasted milk. She swallowed it, coughing.

She looked up at me and gave me her very first look of betrayal.

Well, we were there. We were doing it. Why not press on? She opened her mouth to cry, and I shot some more milk in. She cried even harder, but she was swallowing it.

The silent house echoed with her cries. The cats, sensing something strange and frightening was going down, vacated the upstairs. And when it was all over I was crying, too. I had managed to shoot a whole ounce of milk in there, though, and she had swallowed it. I thought she looked stronger, less drained from hunger. I picked her up, rocked her in my arms, and apologized until she finally stopped crying.

THE HAPPY ENDING

i only had to force-feed Natasha a couple more times. She started to eat a little bit on her own. I started mixing in formula with the milk, having heard that a variety of flavors sometimes helps—it seems that some babies are offended by the prospect of tasting breast milk coming out of a strange and unfamiliar vessel.

After about a week I was able to feed her just fine. I learned that the sight of my face was disturbing to Natasha while she was eating. In other words, my mug was ruining her appetite. I learned to get around the problem by feeding her in the bouncy seat while holding one of her favorite toys between us. This is how all of Natasha's early meals came to be enjoyed while staring raptly into the face of Mr. Fuzzy.

Learn from my travails, my brothers. It might be bottle refusal, it might be problems with naps, it might be a pathological hatred for the car seat. At some point, at some time, your baby might present you with a seemingly insoluble crisis.

Be flexible; try to pick up on the signals your baby is giving you. Be kind and caring. Don't get angry. Try every damned thing you can think of to make it better.

As for Natasha's bottle refusal, it was gone after about a week and a half. She didn't starve to death.

Natasha, sweetheart, Daddy's sorry. He did the best he could under the circumstances. You won't remember it, but he always will.

NOW I LOOK LIKE A DADDY

M y friends Gary and Julie had their son, Henry, when Natasha was about four months old. Henry came into the world with a spectacular head of hair which miraculously didn't fall out, instead just turning thicker and thicker as the months wore on. I had known Gary for a little while before Henry came into the picture, and I was really happy to have found someone I liked and found interesting—and who was entering fatherhood at the same time as I was.

At the time they lived just a few blocks from our house. Gary, a musician, scaled back on his work schedule for a few months after Henry was born, and he was frequently home during the day. I was putting in mornings taking care of Natasha, so we tried to get together as often as we could to enjoy the warm weather and get the babies out of the house.

This usually entailed walks around the neighborhood, not infrequently along the idyllic parkway of Lake of the Isles here in the city. I'd walk over to Gary's place, ring the bell, and wait until he appeared with Henry under one arm and his stroller under the other. Then we'd fuss with our respective strollers and babies and diaper bags until we were finally ready.

"Just two manly guys out for a stroller walk in the middle of the day," I'd say to Gary as we turned the corner.

"Two big strong men with their babies," Gary would concur.

I looked forward to these walks all week, and they're some of my favorite memories of Natasha's early life. But you don't often see two men pushing strollers down the street in the middle of the day. Maybe you *should* see it more, but you don't. I watched people in cars reacting to us with, alternately, looks of blank appraisal or indulgent smiles. *How cute,* I could see people thinking.

"So do you think the Timberwolves are going to actually pull it together this year?" I asked one day, posing the rhetorical question that seemed to consume us both that summer.

We talked about basketball, books, Gary's band, my writing projects, the creative process in general. It was deeply gratifying to be taking care of Natasha while actually pondering something other than baby care. Soon enough, though, it was Natasha's nap time.

"I'd better be getting back," I said. Natasha let out a gurgle of mild dissatisfaction from the stroller.

"I'll walk with you," Gary said. We maneuvered our strollers up onto the curb, heading away from the lake.

As we walked down the street, we heard the sound of banging hammers above our heads. Summer in Minnesota is when people replace their roofs. It's like a regional pastime, since almost half the year here is too cold for such projects.

We neared the house that was being worked on. There was a Dumpster full of old shingles parked on the street, and about eight guys up on the roof. They slowed their work as we approached, and before long we were the object of the entire crew's attention.

Gary and I looked up. We nodded at the workers.

"What, are you guys like *Mr. Moms* or something?" one of them shouted down at us.

"Uh . . . something like that," I said.

"So you take care of the babies all day while your wives are at work?" he pressed on. "Cool."

"Well, it's not—" I said weakly.

"We *work*," Gary called up to the roof.

"We're self-employed," I explained, sounding like I was justifying myself.

The crew of roofers looked down at us like we were an exhibit at a carnival. If anything, they seemed to approve. I guess when you're up on a hot roof, living the life of a kept man doesn't seem so bad.

"We work," I repeated as Gary and I forged on with our strollers.

Just two manly men taking a stroller walk in the middle of the day. Nothing to it. And I finally looked like a Daddy to me.

As soon as your child is old enough to hold something in her hands, always make something available to her: a rattle, a rubber ball, a wadded-up napkin. This is great for stroller walks, because the baby has something to do while she's relaxing and taking in the scenery. The baby gets a great charge out of her newfound power, and will be pleasantly occupied with the task of trying to keep the object from falling out of her hand. Try to always keep a familiar object ready in your pocket when you go out; when baby gets bored or irritable, a proffered gift can keep her mood from turning sour.

DO AS I SAY, NOT AS I DO: THE TV DILEMMA

After Natasha was born I turned into even more of a TV junkie than I had been in the first place, as should be apparent by now from my recollections of that time. Even when Natasha reached the point at which she didn't need to be held all the time any more—thus eliminating my excuse for watching—I went on staring at the screen. I was tired and stressed; I needed to let my mind blissfully vegetate. And once you really *get into* TV, it seems as if there's always something good on. Well, *almost* always.

By the time Natasha was four or five months old she was able to watch TV and follow what was going on, in her own way. This meant no more Jerry Springer for me—I didn't want to be responsible for what *that* would do to her mind. Fortunately she liked sports. Lots of people in colorful costumes running around, lots of noise and action. Essentially the same reason I enjoy sports, come to think of it.

But a more serious issue reared its head. I heard about a national study which suggested that too much TV watching was bad for kids. It was bad for their attention span, their social skills, their development in general.

I can sum up my reaction to this study in one word: *duh*. Take a look at yourself after about an hour of flatlining in front of *Nash Bridges*. You're zombified. You're slouching. There's a pool of drool at your feet. Your eyes hurt, but you can't stop looking.

Americans watch too much TV. *I* watch too much TV. I'm not proud of it, but it's the truth. And when Natasha's eighteen and lives under her own roof, then *she* can watch too much TV. But until then . . .

Once your child is old enough to enjoy TV, it's pretty tempting to park her in front of the tube indefinitely. You can have a cup of coffee, read the paper, scratch your feet. Or you can sit and stare at *Teletubbies* right along with your offspring. But resist the impulse to leave her there all morning.

By the time Natasha was ten months or so, she had certain modes in which she would have probably watched TV until she fell asleep from exhaustion. My first impulse was to say *That's my girl, chip off the old block*. But then responsibility set in and I had to turn the thing off. I dragged her to the park, where she looked around mystified: *I know Tinky Winky's around here someplace*.

Babies *love Teletubbies*. I don't mind it myself. The plots come across like they were cooked up during a prolonged hallucinogenic experiment at a desert commune, and the fact that they play those short films in the middle of the show *twice* can feel like a blessing and a curse from one moment to the next. But it's gentle fun, and it is expressly designed to captivate and entertain babies. I have *SportsCenter* and Natasha has *Teletubbies*. All is right in the world.

It's all a matter of setting boundaries. I try to limit Natasha to half an hour of TV in the morning, an hour at the most. Half a *Barney* and a full *Teletubbies,* for instance. Then no more TV until nighttime, when I might pull out a video for her if she needs to chill out. You'll have to determine for yourself and your child what these limits should be. Just remember that your baby needs to experience the world, not the endless void of staring at the tube. And, in general, PBS children's shows are better. Most of the kids' shows on commercial TV are little more than advertisements for action dolls, and you really don't want to watch your child spacing out in front of commercials—most of which are designed to portray parents as dull-witted, semianimate dispensers of money, food, and gifts (whether or not this viewpoint will turn out to be true is a matter best left untouched).

I would suggest the same for you, but I don't want to sound like a hypocrite. Just pass the *TV Guide* and dim the lights.

BUILD THAT BRAIN

research indicates that a critical amount of brain development in humans takes place in the first two years of life. *But that's right now for my child!*

Don't panic. Do keep in mind, however, that your baby is making neurological connections right now, and you can help. The most important thing is to connect with her: talk to her, sing to her, hold her, look into her eyes and try to make her smile. The worst thing you can do for your baby's development is to not pay enough attention to her.

Keep structured activities simple. Get out a few household objects—make sure they're big enough not to be a choking hazard, since they'll inevitably end up in the baby's mouth. Give them to her and see if she can hand them back. Put a plastic cup within a cup, remove it, hand it over and see if she can do the same. The real secret of playing with babies is that, given the chance, they'll take the lead and start manipulating their environment. Our job is to provide a relaxed atmosphere in which they can explore their developing capabilities.

Be silly. Put a plastic spoon on your nose. Put a ball on your knee and act shocked when the baby knocks it off. Just make sure to interact with your baby every chance you get, and to have fun in the process.

VENTURING OUT OF THE CULTURAL WASTELAND

3abies are usually as amenable to books as they are to TV. And they don't stare at books with slack jaws and drool pouring out of their mouths, which makes reading a more attractive entertainment option—literally.

Read to your child. It's good for her brain development, and it's a way for you to spend time close to her. She'll relax, soothed by the sound of your voice, and you can enjoy her company for a while. Snuggle her in your lap and read her a board book. Point at the pictures, make animal noises. Her eyes are going to widen as, for the moment, you're the greatest entertainer in the world. Linger over the pictures; don't be in a hurry to turn the page.

Once a baby is old enough to hold a book, generally restrict her to board books, unless you can deal with having her rip your library to shreds. Board books are also self-selecting—they tend to be titles based more on pictures than words, with colors and shapes to keep babies interested.

Babies will start to develop favorite books, as you'll be able to tell from your child's reaction. Natasha has gone through a series of favorites—one week it's the book with the animals, the next it's the one with the little balloon that appears in every picture. I started showing her books and reading to her when she was a week old and strapped into her bouncy seat. It's paid off. Now at least a half hour of storytime and book reading is an integral part of her bedtime chill-out routine.

It's also a good idea for your child to see you reading, especially when she gets old enough to know what's going on. Hold your baby in your lap while you read the morning paper and have

your coffee. Point out the pictures and tell her what they are—
don't worry if she can't understand you. Remember that though
you may verbally encourage reading, your message will tend to
be undermined a bit if you spend the better part of each evening
spacing out in front of *Friends* reruns.

A DEFENSE OF BARNEY, AND A CASE FOR POSITIVITY

Let's face it, Barney takes a lot of shit. He's held up as an object of scorn and ridicule by cynical fathers everywhere, and he
inevitably endures the derision of children who have grown up
and become too world-weary for their former dinosaur friend.
It's a wonder the poor bastard hasn't taken the money and run,
crawled into a slough of bitterness and invective directed toward
all these ingrates.

The critics say Barney is insipid; the songs are bland; the
sentiments are stupefying homilies; the kids are mincing little
hams—and don't even get them started on Baby Bop.

I disagree, except for the part about Baby Bop, who is irre-
deemably annoying.

I feel compelled to rise to Barney's defense. The songs are
catchy and simple, and you can sing along with them to entertain
your baby. The prevailing values of the program are friendship,
affection, cooperation, equality, and respect. What the hell's
wrong with that? Have we become so cynical that we dismiss an
innocent children's program that has been put together so that
kids can have a good time and learn a few simple things?

Well, maybe we have. Sometimes I can be as cynical as the
worst of us. But Barney was made for *children*. We have *Larry
Sanders* and *Homicide: Life on the Street* reruns to confirm our
view of the world as full of liars, hubris, and hostility. It behooves
us to give our children at least a few years of innocence before
they're dragged down with the rest of us.

This is a good moment to discuss a general rule of thumb that becomes more and more true starting at the age of about six months old:

THE KID UNDERSTANDS A LOT MORE THAN YOU MIGHT THINK.

Even as tiny infants, children are very perceptive of their parents' moods and attitudes. This is why it's very important to be as cheerful and loving as you can at all times. Even a six-week-old can sense disapproval, anger, and tension in her parents, and as you can imagine, she'll have a hard time dealing with it.

You don't have to tiptoe through the tulips all the time, and you don't have to turn into Chuckles the Clown whenever you're in the presence of your child. But don't be lulled into thinking that the kid is oblivious to what you're doing and saying. She isn't. She's watching you very carefully, taking her cues about the state of the world and her place in it. It's important that she sees you for who you are, with a full range of feelings and a life of your own. At the same time, when she's in the car seat and you're snarling and swearing at all the other drivers on the road, she's back there wondering what the problem is and what it has to do with her.

Which brings us back to Barney. When I learned that Barney was beat up a few years ago by a gang of teenagers (it's true, it happened), I felt bad for any kids who heard about it. By the way, *I know* it was just a guy in a costume. But it's the symbolism that matters. There's enough negativity and hostility in the world without bringing it into the realm of small children. Each blow against Barney is a strike against the gentle values of compassion and love that Barney . . .

Now *stop laughing.* I'm being *serious.*

I realized how much Natasha took her cues from me very early on, when she was a few months old and Sarah and I were arguing. The baby was watching us, her mouth open, a look of perplexed shock on her face. The two most important people in her world were *fighting*. What could this mean? All of a sudden, her place in the universe was far less secure than it had been a moment before.

You can't protect your children from the world forever, but you *can* protect them from *you*. This means that you should try to be more relaxed, calm, fair, and kind in your dealings with her and with the world at large. When you do this, you project security for your baby, and you make the world she's growing up in a place where she can grow and thrive.

And you become a better person in the process. Each of us harbors an angry, irritable, aggressive jerk inside us. Because we're *men*. But now you have a chance to let your child broaden your world and help you improve yourself.

It's another thing you can thank her for later. She'll look at you like you're insane, of course, but at least you'll feel better as you're handing over the car keys.

EXITING THE LAIR

O K, so you finally turned off the TV. It's really important to get out of the house when you have a baby. *No problem,* you might think. But I'm not talking about heading out to the nearest sports bar to watch the NFL playoffs. I'm talking about the whole family getting out: you, your spouse, and the baby.

Between naps, meals, diaper changes, and random minor emergencies, it's pretty easy to fill the day. Even now, on a typical Saturday we might not get Natasha out of her sleeper suit and into proper clothes until eleven or even noon. By then we're all exhausted and it's pretty tempting to pop in a *Teletubbies* tape and recline on the sofa for a while.

You *must* resist this impulse. For one thing, you'll go stir-crazy. As the baby gets older and more aware, she will, too. She needs stimulation and fresh air—and so do you.

Climate can be a problem. When Natasha was a newborn and Sarah was on maternity leave, it was the dead of winter here in Minneapolis. There was one cozy stretch when the temperatures hovered around or fell below zero every day. The world was frozen white. My house made me think of Superman's Fortress of Solitude: a remote hideout deep in icy nothingness. Obviously, it was time to get out.

In those early days a lot of the burden fell on Sarah. She tried to clear out of the house to give me space in which to work. I was so fried from sleep deprivation it was hard enough to find my office at the end of the hall, much less try to write a coherent sentence. But I had to try. The holidays had come and gone, and I was getting my usual early-year fear of failure and pennilessness.

It was too cold to go for a walk, too cold to do much of anything but run for the car and curse softly until the heater kicked in. Sarah took Natasha to the library; she took her to the grocery store. One morning, stir-crazy and craving exercise, Sarah took newborn Natasha to a big shopping mall and pushed her around. Natasha cried and fussed, people stared, and Sarah reached her emotional low point of the postpartum period. That afternoon I found Sarah sobbing in bed next to Natasha's inert form. For a terrible instant I thought something had happened to the baby. Fortunately nothing had. The baby was sleeping, and her mother was having a breakdown.

Well, no one said it was going to be easy. Certainly *I* didn't.

Take the baby out every chance you get. Even in bad weather we make sure to take Natasha someplace at least once a day. When Natasha was tiny she might fall asleep in her stroller, enabling us to have a cup of coffee at Starbucks while staring into space like war refugees. Ah, *the memories.*

Babies have all different kinds of temperaments, and different capacities for handling a variety of situations. You won't know your baby's limits until you try different things. It's easy to use your child as an excuse never to go out, but you have to resist this trap. Remember, you are still living your own life.

A few times during Natasha's first year, we took her to visit our friends Chris and Teddie, who were kind enough to offer to cook dinner for us.

The first time, Natasha was so small she spent much of the evening draped over my shoulder, a position that she seemed to like because it kept constant pressure on her abdomen and enabled her to realize her maximum farting potential. I remember having a drink with Chris and saying something like "I'm functioning at about sixty percent. No, make that *sixty-five*. Why not be optimistic?"

Later on, Natasha was getting stronger and developing more personality. She could crawl around on the floor for at least a minute or two before bonking her face on something and bursting into tears. Chris cooked, and Sarah and I felt like we had a normal social life for a couple of hours.

Teddie became an aunt to Natasha, buying her thoughtful gifts and generally making friends with the young *czarina*. She and Chris were always considerate about having us over to eat earlier than they normally did, so that we could get Natasha home in time for bed. Having friends like them picked us up when we might have felt isolated or depressed.

Some couples hire sitters every weekend and go out together. There's nothing wrong with this. It's very healthy. We didn't do it much, and still don't, primarily because Sarah feels she wants to spend as much time with Natasha as possible after a week spent at work missing her.

Others find it easy to take their babies pretty much anywhere they go. The baby has to be pretty adaptable, and I think the attitude of the parents contributes a lot as well. Sarah and I are not what you would call particularly laid-back people. Gary and Julie took Henry to restaurants when he was less than a month old. Henry has been an exceptionally well-adjusted and easygoing baby, and Gary and Julie have been comfortable and relaxed as parents.

It simply depends on the situation, and the baby. Gary and

Julie came over to dinner one night when Henry was about three months old. Henry crashed out and slept in a playpen in the dining room while, all around him, people talked, drank, and made noise. Nothing bothered little Henry. This will be a skill that will come in handy when he lives in a college dormitory.

However it works, make plans and get out. Hire a sitter, bring the baby with you, just *drop in* to a friend's house or a party if that's all the three of you are up for. Invite people over for coffee on Sunday morning. Now that you have a baby, you're going to have to make more of an effort to stay in touch with your friends and the outside world.

And don't worry. They rerun *SportsCenter* later in the night, after you get home and the kid's gone to bed. You won't miss a thing.

Life in the Sick Ward

When Your Baby Doesn't Feel Well

Your baby is going to get sick; it's sad but true. And for small children even minor illnesses can be pretty traumatic. They don't know how to blow their noses when they're congested, they don't know what a headache is or that it will pass eventually, and they don't have a way to convey to us when something's hurting or feeling uncomfortable.

You can, however, generally tell when babies are sick. They cry for no apparent reason; their eating patterns get thrown off; they can't go to sleep. For most childhood illnesses, you can only try to deal with the symptoms and hope to make the baby feel better until the storm passes. First you should make sure that her symptoms aren't indicative of anything serious. If they aren't, breathe a sigh of relief and wait for better days.

IS IT A COLD OR IS IT THE PLAGUE?

i t's inevitable, and it usually sneaks up on you. Your child seems listless, a little more quiet than usual. Then you notice that she's coughing, or else she erupts with a geyser of vomit from out of nowhere. She starts squirming and crying, she doesn't want food, and nothing you do seems to help.

Babies get sick. Some of them get sick a lot. And there are few things more gut-wrenching than watching your child suffer without being able to do anything about it. All you can do is be prepared to deal with your baby's illness and have the resources ready to determine whether or not the situation is serious.

If you could go to your average day-care center wearing goggles that exposed all the contagious viruses and bacteria spewing from little noses and being rubbed around by little hands, you'd run screaming out of there and immediately immerse yourself from the neck down in antibacterial soap, snarling every time someone tried to hoist you out. We're all exposed to communicable diseases every day, of course, but for the most part adults don't wipe our runny noses on our hands and shove our fingers into our friends' mouths. At least I *hope* we don't.

Not putting your child in day care isn't going to ensure that she doesn't get sick either. She's exposed to all the same things the rest of us are, including the ones that you bring home from the outside world. Because you're so intimate with your child— holding her, kissing her, changing her diapers—you'll be living in optimal conditions for the transmission of diseases.

And here's a secret: it's a two-way street. Now you know why the guys at the office who have children seem to *always* suffer from a cold or some other manner of exotic bowel-impacting, stomach-turning disease that probably should only be dealt with by trained professionals in biohazard suits.

You're living in a petri dish now, my friend. And there's not much you can do about it. Take vitamin C every day, and wash your hands a lot. I don't know if antibacterial soap works, but I use it—despite my lingering fears that I'm helping to breed antibacterial-resistant supergerms that will lay me even lower than the ones I'm fending off. I've never been much of a germophobe, but after having a pale-faced child at Natasha's day care tell me in a weak voice about how *cold* he was—even though the furnace was working fine—I've started to change my ways.

Babies have hard days. Sometimes it's hard to say why, and we might never know. They might have a headache, their lunch might not have agreed with them, or else they—like us—don't really know themselves why they're in such a rotten mood.

For Natasha's first year, her big challenges were getting her sleep regulated, day care, learning to act on her new motor skills, and dealing with mealtime. All of these activities have evolved—or, sometimes, *devolved*—depending on her development and simply the patterns of how things are going. Sometimes things are smooth, sometimes they aren't.

It can really break your heart when you see that your baby is having a rough time. You can see frustration in her cries, anger in her face. Sometimes she'll look at you as though to say *Why aren't you doing anything to help me?* Sometimes you'll be able to help her, sometimes you won't. All you can do is keep a big-picture view and try to stay relaxed. Distract her, hold her, most of all sympathize with her. Babies are just like us: sometimes they want nothing more than to feel like someone understands and cares.

TALES FROM THE SICK WARD

N atasha's had a few illnesses, none of them serious. But the first episode was pretty scary. Natasha was about two months old when I started to feel strange one night. My throat hurt and a weird sort of headache was creeping in from around my eye sockets. I felt cold, so I took a hot shower. When I stepped out of the shower, I started to shiver uncontrollably. About an hour later I was in bed, wiped out, feeling as sick as I could ever remember being.

By the next morning Sarah had it, too. It was a bad flu, the kind that makes it a supreme effort to get up off the couch. Eating is next to impossible. It becomes daunting to take care of *yourself,* much less someone else. And this time it was different— this time we had a baby to contend with, a little person who needed constant attention and vigilance and who (we realized with creeping horror) was probably going to catch this thing from us within a matter of hours.

Here's the good news, and a pretty compelling argument for continuing breast-feeding: a breast-fed baby receives antibodies in mother's milk. Which meant that Sarah's milk was feeding Natasha the molecular stuff she needed to fight off the flu. She got sick—a little sniffly, kind of lethargic—but she was nowhere as incapacitated as we were. Which was a very good thing, be-cause I remember it was three days before either of us was even well enough to leave the house to forage for sustenance.

Another scary moment came when Natasha was a week away from her first birthday. She'd had a cold for a few days and started to develop a hacking cough. We were worried about her, and she required a lot of holding in Sarah's lap and an inordinate amount of time watching PBS's daytime kids' offerings, but she was basically fine. We took her outside so she could watch me hang up Christmas lights on the front of our house.

At first she was laughing and smiling, checking out the lights, grunting and pointing to let us know that she wanted to touch them. But then she turned quiet. When I was done with the lights we all went inside. Natasha crawled over to her toys and pulled herself up to stand. I went over to check her out.

Without warning—and this is one of the worst realities, the fact that before kids can talk it's extremely hard to know precisely what's wrong with them—Natasha lost it. She opened her mouth and puked up her entire lunch. Fried egg, waffle, pears: out it came, all over her and the rug. Then came the bile. Natasha was all right at first, but when more and more came out she looked at Sarah and me with a scared expression and started to cry.

I apologize for being so graphic—especially if you were eating fried eggs and waffles when you were reading the preceding paragraph—but these are the kinds of things you're going to have to deal with. Natasha was crying, she felt hot; we had cleanup to do, and fast. The truth descended on us that Natasha was *really* sick. Then, naturally, Sarah came down with the same thing about twenty-four hours later. I was spared, for some mysterious reason—like the doctor in Camus's *The Plague,* wandering among the sick and afflicted, musing on the meaning of my inscrutable good fortune.

Watching your baby get sick is one of the most difficult aspects of fatherhood. You feel helpless, you feel sometimes like you don't know what to do, and a lot of the time you're sick as well. Here are a few tips gleaned from experience that will help you:

• **Prepare the medicine cabinet.** Stock a few items in one central location to have on hand when your child gets sick.

—Infants' Tylenol and generic equivalents are available in liquid form dispensed with a dropper. This is good for fever and general aches and pains, and Natasha seems to actually like the taste of it.

—Make sure you have a working thermometer and a bulb syringe that you use to suck the snot out of the child's nose. (Good luck. Try it on yourself for endless amusement.) You can also get a baby-friendly version of mentholated rub for your baby's chest when she's suffering from congestion. Think about getting a humidifier for nasal infections, although depending on what kind of heat you have and what kind of climate you live in, you might not need one.

—Antigas medicine for babies is really effective when they're newborns and seem to always have gas pain.

The difficult fact to come to terms with is that there's often nothing you can do when the baby gets sick, other than comfort her and wait for things to get better. Little babies are too small to take Sudafed. And they're generally too little to understand how to blow their noses, so congestion can become a major obstacle to rest and peace. Get out that bulb syringe and try it again. Quit playing with it on yourself, at least until your daughter feels better.

• **Have a plan.** Write down your child's insurance number, along with your health-care provider's phone number, and put it on the refrigerator. Usually you can call up and speak to a nurse, describe your baby's symptoms, and get good advice. Sometimes it's helpful to talk to a professional, just for your own peace of mind. When your daughter is running a fever, with a cough and runny nose, and she won't stop crying, it's going to cross your mind that maybe you should take her to see a doctor. Talking to a nurse can help you determine what you need to do.

Know where to find the emergency room at your hospital. There's also often a middle ground between a doctor's visit and the emergency room, such as an after-hours care facility you can access by making an immediate appointment.

One time when Natasha was about six months old she woke up screaming from a nap at about five in the afternoon. She was inconsolable after about half an hour of crying and, though she was showing no sign of being hurt or sick, she was scaring the shit out of us. It was a weekend, so we called up the after-hours care number and brought her in right away. By the time we got there, she'd stopped crying, and she smiled and charmed the nursing staff and the doctor—who suggested that maybe she had had a nightmare, because there was certainly nothing wrong with her.

Which brings us to another important point: abandon your pride. You might look like a hand-wringing worrier for bringing your son to the doctor because he's got a spot on his back, but at least *call* the doctor if you're concerned. Looking foolish beats overlooking a real health problem.

If you don't have health insurance, make sure you're in touch with social-service agencies and local clinics. Know what you can do in an emergency, and who you can call for free advice. Take it from me: you don't want to have to figure out logistics when your child is really sick.

- **Keep your head on straight.** Your child is taking most of her cues in life from you and her mother. If she's sick, the last thing she needs is to feel out of control because you're panicking. Children are pretty sturdy, so take control of the situation and keep telling her that she's going to be all right. Children are little humans, but one of the big differences between them and us is that they can't communicate with words. Imagine having a splitting headache and not being able to do anything about it, *and* not being able to tell anyone what's the matter. Frustration builds on discomfort, and pretty soon it's hard to stop crying. You'll realize again how hard it is to be a baby.

Dealing with your child's illnesses is one of the hardest things about fatherhood. Maybe it helps now to learn a lesson:

YOU CAN'T CONTROL EVERYTHING.

Sometimes your kid is going to be sick. She's going to get bad flus, throw up, and she might even break a bone someday. Protect her the best you can without stifling her, and take care of her when she isn't feeling well. Remember not to beat yourself up because you can't make the world perfect for her. No one can, not even you.

Also keep in mind that babies can exhibit symptoms that would alarm an adult, but which are perfectly normal for them.

A few examples:

🐌 **1. Weird shit** is normal. Breast-fed babies tend to shit every time they eat, while formula-fed babies might go less often. As they get older, the material they produce can vary more. To be frank, you might be too attuned to your daughter's bowel movements because you're the one cleaning up after them. If the baby's stools are hard and dry a few times in a row, she's probably constipated. Diarrhea is another concern. These two problems may merit a call to the doctor. Also, obviously, the presence of blood is a warning sign.

🐌 **2. Spitting up** is also routine. Keep in mind that what looks like a lot of vomit is probably only an ounce or so. Make sure that you push the air out of the bottle while feeding, and keep the baby upright for a few minutes after you feed her.

If you're worried about the amount your baby is spitting up, try a demonstration that might ease your fears. Pour into a glass a volume of water equal to your child's typical feeding: let's say four ounces. Now pour the water over a towel or splash it into the sink. It looks like a lot, doesn't it? Sometimes a spectacular puking episode only *looks* dire and worrisome—in most cases the child is just spitting up a couple of ounces.

🐌 **3. Babies cough** to clear out their airways. Don't worry too much unless she also has a fever or has problems eating and sleeping.

🐌 **4. Crying is how they communicate.** Not all crying means that something's wrong. Life is hard for a baby, and sometimes crying is their only means of expression. Ride out the storm, and don't worry too much, as long as your baby is showing no obvious signs of illness.

Visits to the doctor can be nothing short of grueling for parents and babies alike. Sometimes it's fine—the baby seems to enjoy the pediatrician and the inevitable mobiles hanging from the ceiling. Other times it's a short trip on greased rails to hell.

If you get your child vaccinated, be prepared for the sight of a medical technician inserting a big needle into a tender spot on your child's body, then the inevitable yell of pain and outrage. It's usually at precisely this moment that the baby finds you in the room, locks eyes with you, and shoots you a look of bottomless hurt and betrayal. If you throw up your hands as if to say *What can I do? It's for your own good,* then the cries will intensify. Pick up the baby and console her. It'll be better soon.

One time we took Natasha to the pediatrician's for a routine visit. As though she'd known what was coming, Natasha had skipped her afternoon nap at day care and was on the verge of exhaustion by the time we reached the doctor's office. Then we had to wait almost half an hour to see the doctor, during which time the baby became hungry and irritable. Sarah and I exchanged anxious looks. The *czarina* was restless.

We stripped her down to be weighed, and she cried. Then she got a shot, which made her cry even harder. Her head drooped with fatigue and hunger, and long streams of tears fell down her cheeks. There was only one more thing to be done that visit, we were told. We had to take the baby into the next room so that she could have some blood drawn in order to check her iron levels. Another technician was waiting with a small vial and a scary needlelike implement.

"Hold her hand still," he said. "I'm going to need to prick her finger with this."

"OK," I said. What I thought was: *you have to be shitting me.*

Poke! The needle pierced Natasha's finger, and she let out a howl. She squirmed and screamed as Sarah and I held her still. Then the technician *squeezed* big drops of blood out of the baby's finger into the plastic vial. Natasha shuddered, fought, whimpered, then finally gave up. It was all too much for her.

And she wasn't even old enough to get a lollipop for her trouble when it was finally over.

THE SPAGHETTI INCIDENT

Natasha was about eight months old. The world was her playground. As long as she was fed and rested, she was relentlessly upbeat and she regarded the world as a place of beaming faces and a limitless supply of fascinating objects to explore and manipulate.

The baby thing: When it's going well, it's totally transcendent and will color your life with shades and hues that you never imagined were possible. My daughter can get on a *roll*, and when she does, I wish that for a second I could live inside her mind and see the world as she does.

One summer night we were having a great family time. My daughter had a cold, but she wasn't letting it get her down. She was sniffling and snotty, but she was taking it with typical good humor.

Natasha had a normal dinner—baby-food sweet potatoes, some Monterey Jack cheese. For a new wrinkle, we gave her some of the spaghetti that Sarah and I were eating that night. We served it to her without sauce—astringent tomato can be too much for a young baby's digestive system. Natasha didn't know the difference, and she hungrily consumed about a dozen strands that we had overcooked and sliced into lengths of a few inches each.

The end of dinnertime was signaled by Natasha's carefully picking up bits of her food and dropping them to the floor from the lofty height of her high-chair seat. At first this was a little annoying—who wants to get down on his knees and handpick food bits off a hardwood floor? But we started to realize that she was helping out, having learned that cleanup is what we do at the end of a meal. So Natasha, her tongue stuck out between her lips in intense concentration, was busying herself with a little tidying up. Sarah lifted her out of the high chair, and we went outside to enjoy the evening.

This was my favorite time of day, the window between dinner and bath time. I would sit on the stoop while Sarah carried Natasha around the yard and inspected the garden. Our roses were doing well, and the hops we had planted beneath the arch in front of our house had taken root and were starting to climb. I sat and watched people walking by, and generally felt grateful to have my little oasis in the city.

Sarah was looking strangely at Natasha, I noticed, but I didn't think much of it. I stretched out my legs and pondered what I was going to do that night. I barely noticed when Sarah gestured for me to join them on the sidewalk.

"What's up?" I asked.

"Look up her nose," Sarah said, a note of uncertainty in her voice.

OK, I thought, *why not?* Things were going so well. Maybe there was something wonderful up my little flower's nose.

"What's that?" I said.

I saw a little piece of *something* way up there in Natasha's perfectly round nostril. The baby started to complain and writhe.

"I hope it's not what I think it is," Sarah said.

I felt my smile freeze on my face. "And what would that be?"

Sarah lifted Natasha up in the air, looked into the baby's nose like a scientist proving a particularly troubling hypothesis.

Then she let Natasha settle into her arms. As soon as things were back to normal, Natasha started smiling again.

"Maybe I'm crazy," Sarah said. "But it looks like a piece of spaghetti stuck up there."

"No!" I said, laughing.

Apparently things weren't quite as tranquil in babyworld as we had thought. I had Sarah hold Natasha up again, and realized she was right. Way up there in her nostril was the blunt end of a piece of pasta.

"How the hell'd it get up there?" I asked, amazed.

"Beats me."

Over the course of the intervening minutes, my wife and I applied our deductive skills and came up with a hypothesis.

(Deductive skills, by the way, will come in very handy for you in your capacity as a father. You're going to become a baby detective, taking a set of bizarre circumstances and trying to figure out how they came to pass. You're going to be very impressed with how varied and unpredictable this thing we call reality can be.)

Here's what we knew: *Natasha had a strand of spaghetti up her nose.* A second piece of information was very crucial: *Natasha had a cold.*

There was only one possibility: Natasha, in the course of eating her spaghetti that evening, had managed to suck a strand of it up the back of her throat, probably while in the process of snorting up the snot that was even at this moment running down her upper lip. As though concurring with our speculation, Natasha ran her tongue over her lip, got a taste of snot, then snorted it back up into her nose.

"Imagine that," I said. "It seems impossible."

But, see, there's really no such thing as *impossible*. Not when you're dealing with a small child.

"What now?" I asked. "Do you think it'll come out on its own?"

"Well, I certainly *hope* so," Sarah said. "But we can't count on that happening, can we?" Sarah asked.

"I guess not."

Natasha was oblivious. In her world, I supposed, having a strand of pasta stuck up your sinus cavity was pretty much par for the course.

"Well, let's give her a bath," Sarah said.

This particular bath time was not entirely the jolly, relaxing experience that it was at its best. That little strand of spaghetti had taken up residence in my consciousness. Natasha had her usual postbathing attack of fatigue, and we put her in her crib. She crashed out with no protest, and when we turned on the baby monitor we heard only the soothing sound of her lullaby tape.

We decided to call the twenty-four-hour baby hot line number that we'd received from the hospital. We were probably overreacting, we figured. This kind of thing probably happened all the time.

Oh, your baby will be fine, we expected to hear. *Just let her sleep and everything will be peachy in the morning.*

Instead, the reaction went something like this: "What? She did *what*? Oh my goodness. I'm going to call the doctor at home and ask him what to do. You're going to have to bring her in to urgent care."

Urgent care? Like the emergency room?

We got a call back within five minutes—an ominous sign. The words *medical emergency* flitted through my mind.

"Bring her to the hospital," the nurse who called us back said. "We have a slot for you at eight o'clock. And, for future reference, your daughter is too young to be eating spaghetti. The doctor said so."

At times like these, some of your truisms will conflict. Taking Natasha to the hospital meant waking her from her evening slumber. But, I thought, what about *never wake a sleeping baby*? I did what any computing machine would do after receiving conflicting instructions: I broke down, smoke floating out of my ears.

And another thing: What was this business about not giving Natasha pasta? Her pediatrician had said it was OK. And she had *liked* it. The only problem was the fact that she had inhaled some of it. Happens to the best of us. This was when I fell back on a real truism of fatherhood: *You don't have to take or believe every bit of advice you receive.*

"I'll go get her," Sarah said. "You get the car ready or something."

"Right!" I said, grabbing for the keys. Time to *take charge.* When Sarah came down with Natasha I felt a lot better. The baby seemed amused by this unusual turn of events. Get up out of bed and go somewhere after bedtime? *Why not?* she seemed to be thinking.

We drove to the same hospital where Natasha was born. The desk staff was expecting us when we arrived, and we were ushered straight back to a treatment room. We had to explain the situation to the doctor several times before he got a handle on it.

"OK," he said, probably using the voice he reserved for deranged mental patients. "Well, let's have a look."

The doctor confirmed our diagnosis. *Spaghetti in the sinuses.* He looked at me, Sarah, and the nurse. "You'll have to hold her down," he said.

At first I wondered to whom he was talking, then I realized: *all three of us.* An eight-month-old baby has an incredible amount of squirm power, and it was going to take three adults to hold her still.

The doctor took out a pair of tweezers. Natasha started to squall on the table, impervious to our assertions that everything was going to be all right soon.

"Phrawwwwww!" Natasha exclaimed.

"Hmm," the doctor said as he put the tweezers very deep in my daughter's nose. I had a weird and terrible memory of an image from my childhood: when Egyptians mummified their kings, they removed the brains through the nose, using a long hook. I really, *really* hoped that no brains were going to come out with that noodle.

But brains *looked* like noodles, didn't they? What if something came out and we couldn't tell what it was? Noodle or brain: Who would be qualified to know the difference? Maybe we needed a brain surgeon.

I tried to take a deep breath. *OK, get a grip.*

"This isn't working," the doctor said. He pulled out the tweezers, let Sarah pick up Natasha to comfort her.

"Well, what's next?" I asked. I had images of invasive procedures, scarring. Natasha in elementary school, laughed at by the other children because of the long mark on her face left from emergency pasta-removal surgery.

"This," the doctor said. He had a little metal device, with a long handle and a loop at the end. He opened and closed it experimentally, then said, "We'll need to hold her down again. Hold her *very still.*"

Easier said than done. Natasha let out a howl of betrayal. Her brown eyes scanned the room as her fear escalated into panic.

"*Huhhhrrrrawwwwl!*" Natasha said.

The doctor tried once, failed. Frustration played over his features. He put the long instrument back in Natasha's nostril, and after about thirty seconds made a little sound of satisfaction.

"Got it," he said.

And then he pulled it out, very slowly. It was, indeed, a length of cooked spaghetti, about three inches long.

"You'll want to keep this as a souvenir," the doctor said. He put the offending object in a tissue and handed it to me. Sarah picked up Natasha again; the baby instantly stopped crying and, a moment later, was flirting with the nurse.

All was well. I felt like hugging the doctor but decided that it probably wouldn't be received in the spirit with which it was intended. On the way out, Natasha was loving life again. She smiled at the nurses at their station, princess of the world once more.

"By the way," I asked the doctor. "You've seen this before, right? I mean, this kind of thing happens all the time."

The doctor looked at me closely, trying to see if I was putting him on.

"Nope," he said. "Never seen this one before. How about you?" he asked the nurse.

"Never," she said. "You're the first."

I still have the piece of pasta the doctor extracted from my daughter's nose. It's on top of my computer monitor, right next to a framed picture of her taken at about two months old. It will occupy a place of honor until such time as I deem her responsible enough to take possession of it. It has become one of our first family heirlooms.

11

Domestic Bliss

Arranging Your Child's Care for When You're Not Around, and Dealing With the Mess You Come Home To

Now you have a child, and she's beginning to grow up. She's no longer a newborn. She has a sense of humor, she's almost ready to become mobile, and she loves her dad. Congratulations. It couldn't have happened to a better guy. By now you've probably noticed something about the nature of babies: they have to be cared for *all the time, every minute of the day.* You can't go out for a cup of coffee, man, not without leaving her with someone or taking her with you. It's a heavy reality, and if you and your partner are both working you're going to have to find some sort of stable day-care solution that fits your and your baby's needs.

It's a lot to sort out, and at the end of the day you just want to relax and read the paper. If you can find it. You might have to settle for reading yesterday's edition, because today's mysteriously disappeared somewhere in the pile of toys and laundry that used to be your living room.

WHAT? THEY'RE NOT GOING TO PAY ME FOR DOING NOTHING?

N ow it's time to think about how you're going to deal with caring for your child after your spouse's maternity leave has ended. The basic principle: *someone* has to be with the child at all times. The question is: *who?*

This is something that you'll be well-served to have thought about in advance. It requires a delicate balance, because inevitably something has to give. Caring for a baby is a twenty-four-hour job—and *someone* is currently spending those twenty-four hours doing something other than taking care of a baby.

After you take a good look at your finances, start to look at your life with an open mind. Is it possible for one of you not to work, or to start working part-time? Would either you or your partner *want* to scale back on work? Can you afford day care? Can you afford *not* to put your child in day care? There are seemingly endless combinations of the work/home dilemma, and each family has to sort them out in the way that works best for them.

Sometimes I think it would be great to devote myself full-time to being with Natasha. I'd still need time to myself, of course, and it would be a challenge, but I think I could make it work.

Of course, we would soon be *homeless*, since our family requires two paychecks to make ends meet.

I know families in which either the mother or the father stays home with the child; these families are lucky enough to be able to get by on one income. I also know families in which both spouses work full-time. There are a lot of points on the line in between. And most of them involve some sort of day care.

Day care is a reality. It involves the proximity of the provider, the type of day care involved, the expense, and the amount of time your child is going to spend there.

The question: How are *you* going to do it? It's time to ask yourself some questions and figure out the logistics of the new regime.

OPEN YOUR CHECKBOOK—
DAY CARE'S CALLING

ⅅay care costs money. It can cost *a hell of a lot* of money. At the very least, you're looking at adding approximately the equivalent of a car payment to your monthly expenses.

There are essentially two kinds of day-care setups: in-home care and centers. In-home care means that someone has set up a space in her house and obtained a license to call herself a day-care provider. She has to answer to the government in terms of how many children she cares for on a daily basis.

A center involves a commercial space, employees, and usually all kinds of extra features. These are the setups that will talk to you about infant-to-care-provider ratios, educational programs, and all the ways that they can customize the day-care environment to suit your baby.

The third possibility is having a family member take on day-care duties—your mother, mother-in-law, maybe even a grandmother. (I don't count male family members because I haven't seen it done. Maybe when our generation is old enough.) Unfortunately, most families I know are so geographically scattered that this isn't possible. I grew up in a working-class neighborhood in Columbus, Ohio. My mother was a secretary, and she had to return to work almost immediately after giving birth to me. She was fortunate enough to have her mother living in the same part of town. My grandmother was a widow, and she agreed to take care of me in exchange for what must have been next to nothing. I remember doing a lot of reading, going for long walks with my grandmother—she loved to walk places—and taking the bus downtown to go shopping. Today my mother lives about a thousand miles away from me, and she works full-time. In a generation, countless social realities have changed.

I found out very quickly after Natasha's birth that day care is one of the hot zones for parents' expectations. Parents can be quite particular about their children's day care, and only a certain kind will suffice. Some day-care centers in my part of south Minneapolis have waiting lists. I don't criticize parents for choosing more elite options—they're simply making the best choice in their estimation. But the kind of day-care center I've just described costs a lot of money. How much? It depends on where you live. You should be willing to part with a *minimum* of six hundred dollars a month to drop your kid off full-time in one of these places. If you live in a big city, count on that figure doubling.

Maybe you can't afford this. I know I can't. When you start looking into day-care scenarios, you might discover pretty quickly that you're priced out of a lot of options. This is reality, my friend. I'm uncomfortable with the way things are, because I think more affluent people use their money to start their children on a path of elitism and social segregation that runs through private schools and continues into an adulthood of being unable to connect with people on all ends of the socioeconomic scale.

But that's just me.

The fact is, we're all doing our best. It's important for you to realize that day-care options are many, and that you need to find a solution that works for you.

I don't remember exactly when it happened, or who came up with the idea, but we realized we could put Natasha in day care for half-days. I could take care of her the other half, thanks to my flexible writing schedule. If I had to, I could work nights in order to pick up the slack.

This was a great solution for us, as we had been hesitant

about day care. We were uncomfortable with leaving Natasha in someone else's care all day. Babies are only awake for about ten hours a day, and full-time day care meant we would get to see Natasha on weekdays for about two hours a day, at best. What's the point of having a child if we never saw her? we figured.

The other reason to avoid full-time day care was that we couldn't afford it. Sarah got a list of local centers from Hennepin County and we started scouting around when Natasha was about a month old. Six hundred dollars a month? Don't make me laugh—or cry. There was no way we were going to be able to come up with that kind of money. We looked at a couple of prestigious day-care centers, like hungry children with their faces pressed against the bakery window. What was inside was fancy, probably sweet and good, but it was out of our reach.

We went down the list, drove by a few, talked to some day-care providers. Some made us feel as if we were applying for a job, rather than trying to hire someone. We thought we had an advantage—we wanted someone to watch over Natasha for only four hours a day. Perversely, it was harder to find part-time day care than full-time. One provider even had the audacity to demand that we pay a full day, saying "A slot is a slot." Yeah, and five hundred bucks is five hundred bucks.

Don't get me wrong. I'm well aware that the people who work in day-care centers aren't driving home at the end of the day in Range Rovers and BMWs. It's difficult, draining, demanding work.

Finally we found something we liked. It was an address just four blocks from our house, meaning we wouldn't have to drive to drop Natasha off. We put her in the Snugli on a cold winter afternoon—I remember that the temperature was around zero—and slogged our way through the snowdrifts and unshoveled sidewalks.

Inside the house was a commotion of child energy. I looked around at all the kids, ranging from toddlers to those of school age. It was winter break, so the kids who were usually gone during the day were pressed in there with all the others. They were playing games, watching TV, coloring, babbling to their toys. Infant Natasha stirred as we pulled her out of my coat, her brown eyes widening to take it all in.

The day-care provider was named Carol; she was a grandmother with a kind face and a playful smile that would show itself for a second or so before retreating. I got an immediate impression of kindness and intelligence from her. We sat down at a table amid the tornado of children, then handed the baby over. Carol's eyes brightened the way only a grandmother's can, and she looked at Natasha with deep fondness.

We talked money and availability. Sarah and I were starting to feel anxious—time was closing in; and we weren't sure we were even going to be able to afford child care. But Carol's rate was very reasonable, and she seemed happy that Natasha would only be there half-days—an infant is so labor-intensive, it's draining to care for one, no matter the setting.

Our decision to start bringing Natasha to Carol was based on proximity and money, to begin with. But it developed into much more. I noticed that the children respected Carol, and behaved respectfully toward each other. I saw a Christmas card taped to a door frame addressed to "Grandma Carol," and indeed, there was a feeling of *family* in the air. I got the sense that the same children had been coming there for a long time—which turned out to be right. The kids all knew each other; they had formed a tight little community that they could enjoy while their parents were out earning a living.

I didn't realize it at the time, but I had learned an important lesson. Your day-care provider is more than someone you pay for a service. They're probably the most important person in your child's life, after you and your partner. Your child is entering into an important relationship, one that he will learn and grow from. So approach day care with that in mind.

A child inevitably bonds with her day-care provider if there's continuity in who she sees every day. Natasha *loves* Carol; she reaches out to embrace her as soon as we arrive every afternoon, and basically treats her like a close family member.

Some people become jealous of this bond; they don't like their children to get too close to their day-care provider. If this sounds like you, *come off it.* This attitude—and it's more common than you think—comes from insecure parents who are worried about how much their children love them. They're too self-centered to realize that their children will always love them most, no matter what, and that the more healthy and loving relationships their child enjoys in life, the better off she'll be.

Just before Natasha's three-month birthday, I loaded her into the Snugli and took her to Carol. The schedule was simple: one until five in the afternoon, Monday through Friday.

There have been good days and bad. *That's* true for all of us. But Natasha has found a second family with whom to spend her afternoons while Daddy is frantically trying to churn out a few pages before the afternoon gets away from him. Sometimes I wonder whether it would be better if we'd found a way for Sarah not to work—certainly there was a time, early on, when she would have been willing. But overall I like the way things have worked out. Natasha has learned independence without having to spend entire days away from her family.

A NEW CAR, OR MORE TIME WITH MY KID?

The way I've found to deal with day care is *my* way. Just because I like it doesn't mean it would be best for you. Maybe you have the money to put your child in full-time, top-line day care, and maybe this is what you're set on doing. Well, more power to you. Maybe you have almost no money at all, and you're looking at finding the cheapest day care around. That's a tough situation, but remember that quality day care can be a result of quality individuals as well as quality surroundings.

It's important to find a solution that fits your life. Spending money you can't afford on a day care just because nine out of ten toddlers from a particular place went on to Harvard doesn't make sense to me. The baseline considerations for day care are: Will my child be taken care of and not neglected? Is there a stimulating social environment, rather than a steady eight-hour diet of TV cartoons? And, once your child has been there for a couple of weeks, does he seem happy?

When you pick up your child at day care and he has a big scratch across his face, take a deep breath before you say anything. Remember that your day-care provider can't be everywhere at once, and that she surely has your child's best interests at heart.

Natasha was bitten and scratched by another young child at her day care. My first thoughts were of angry vengeance, especially after I met the child's father and he didn't offer a word of apology. But then I reminded myself: These things happen. Children fall down, they get bruised, they get roughed up. As long as you feel confident that your day-care provider is keeping an eye on things and policing the interactions between the children, don't worry yourself to death.

It's painful to see your kid with a cut or a bruise, especially when it happened when you weren't around. *If only I'd been there* . . . you might think. But remember all the falls and scrapes that happen at home. It's simple physics: fall down, go boom.

Carol has taken such good care of Natasha that I know my daughter is in trustworthy hands every time I drop her off. More than once when I've brought Natasha with a bruise or a mark on her face, Carol has laughed and said, *I'm always glad when that happens before they get here.* She knows from experience that kids are going to get beat up by the world. From her point of view, it's always better when it doesn't happen on her watch, because she cares about the kids and feels responsible, and also because she knows some parents, in their secret heart, will blame her for anything that happens.

Give your day-care provider a break. We're all doing our best.

Day care is the place where your child can begin to develop social relationships outside the family. Your daughter won't really have friends until she's well more than a year old, but she'll observe the other children and watch them interact. Natasha has learned to hold a crayon from day care, for instance—one day at home she just did it, without me teaching her.

It's important to feel good about leaving your child in day care, but it's also important to realize that a six-month-old doesn't really need a head start on learning and achievement. What he needs is love and security. He needs *you*.

The fact is, day care is a second-best measure—second-best to your child being with you and your partner. It can be a very positive environment, but it isn't better than the home. Anyone who thinks otherwise is fooling himself. Is your child going to learn to work a computer at age two at your day care? Is he going to be fluent in French by the time he's toilet-trained? *Great. Terrific.* We should all have such advantages in life.

But is that better than his spending time with you? No.

For many people, day care is the only option. Your family might need two full-time incomes to make ends meet—mine does. I'm still working full-time, essentially, while also doing half-time day-care duties. It's hard, but I'm lucky enough to have Natasha home half the day.

Sometimes families have a greater range of choice than they want to admit to themselves. I'm talking about couples who both make good money and who have disposable income. Day-care centers are full of kids who have two professional parents, neither of whom is willing to give up their pursuit of career, money, and *self* in order to scale back and spend time with their offspring. You can recognize these children—they're the ones acting crazy in the supermarket on Saturday morning because they're so excited and confused about spending the day with their parents after seeing them for only an hour a day during the week.

Having two Range Rovers, a closetful of expensive suits, and a house full of state-of-the-art TV and stereo equipment, while sending children to full-time day care as both parents work to support their class pretensions and consumer addictions . . . well, in my opinion, it's *wrong*. Your child is more important than a *car*.

Think about it. Maybe this applies to you, maybe it doesn't. Maybe you or your partner would only have to work part-time if you scaled back on your household spending. Put yourself in your child's position; realize how much this would mean to him. If you can make it work, *do it*.

I'm sorry if I've offended your sensibilities. But I see children in the supermarket and the mall with weekend parents too lost in their own ambitions and self-gratification to really think about the needs of the person they brought into the world. I see children foisted off on expensive baby-sitters, and I try to imagine the lessons these children must be learning about life.

Whatever your situation, my brother, make it work. Do the right thing; do the best you can. If you don't, who will?

BLESS THIS MESS

As your son gets old enough to really move around, you're going to notice that the state of housekeeping in your home has deteriorated alarmingly. Toys will be everywhere, there will be ripped-up magazines and tissues—a baby considers *everything* a toy, you will soon discover. Also, you'll be so busy dealing with the baby, and so tired in general, that it will be almost impossible to keep up your home to the standards you might prefer.

If you have the money, hire a cleaning service to come in every week or two. If you're like me, you have to learn to let it wash over you.

Once children are more than a few months old they develop what I call microvision. They all do it. They have an uncanny ability to fixate on the smallest of objects on the ground: bugs, pieces of lint, flecks of things left behind even after an industrial-strength vacuum cleaner has scoured the place.

Pretty soon they develop the ability to pick these objects up. Next they learn to put them in their mouths. Natasha has a telltale expression of confusion and disgust that always alerts me that she has some odd piece of debris in her mouth. *This isn't food,* she's saying. *This isn't anything even approximating food.*

This is when you'll learn to open your child's mouth and fish out the object. They *love* that. (If you've ever had a dog or a cat, you will have had prior experience with this maneuver.) When they get a little older, they learn to spit out the weird bits, then eventually to pick them off their tongues on their own. Natasha reached the point at which she'd been burned so many times that she simply held up the objects for me, as though to say *Here, take this away. This doesn't belong in my playland.*

My brother-in-law Dan says that homicide detectives should have vans full of babies on hand at all times. Then when they need to scour a crime scene in search of microscopic pieces of evidence, they could unleash the babies on the room. It's food for thought—or *nonfood* for thought.

I talked to my friend Ross around the time his daughter Meg was eighteen months old.

"My place is a pigsty," I told him.

"Tell me about it, man." He sighed. "We've put our house on the market, and since I got home tonight we've been trying to clean up. But it's a total disaster. I don't see how anyone is going to want to buy it. You'd need a bulldozer to clear the wreckage."

"If it's anything like mine, they'll take one look at the place and run screaming."

"That's what I'm worried about," Ross replied.

A pause, followed by some strange noises on the line.

"Say hello to Quinton," Ross said.

Silence, then a little elfin voice. "Hello."

"Hello, Meg," I said.

"Hello," she said again.

Ross came back on the phone. "I'm not kidding," he said. "You wouldn't believe this place."

"I'd stack up my mess against yours," I told him. "Is Meg playing with discarded junk mail and greeting cards?"

"All the time," Ross said wearily.

"How about kitchen utensils?" I asked. "Natasha gets ahold of spatulas and plastic cups and won't give them back. They end up scattered around all over the place."

"And the dirty clothes," Ross added. "Not to mention the tissues and the books."

"I know. Natasha likes to empty out the dirty clothes basket and spread underwear and washcloths all over the room."

"They *love* that," Ross moaned.

"The thing is, a messy house makes me nervous," I told him.

"That's right," he concurred. "So you feel a kind of low-level anxiety all the time."

When we hung up, Ross had to go give Meg a bath and get

ready to put her to bed. He and Ann had been working on cleaning the house since Ross got home—after Ross had spent a full day at work and Ann had put in a day caring for Meg. Neither had had time to even sit down.

This is the way it works; there seems to be no getting around it. I will flail about the house, cleaning up little messes, and when I'm done it looks like nothing has changed. I'll hear Sarah in the kitchen cleaning for forty-five minutes; by noon the next day, it looks like the kitchen of a seedy diner.

Kids make messes. You make messes. And now you don't have enough time to clean them all up. Housework becomes a task of Sisyphian dimensions. You just need to roll up your sleeves and do your best. And, at the end of the day, you need to be able to take a breath and let it all go until the sun comes up again.

Baby Chef

The Basics of Feeding Your Child

Taking care of your baby is hard work, but at least for the first few months her menu was easy: formula or breast milk. Before long, though, her needs change. She starts to eat solid foods. If you're like me, you had no idea what children could eat or what they prefer. All I knew was that eating with them was unappetizing, what with their propensity for mashing their food up, playing with it, and rubbing it all over their faces.

The good news: after a while, *nothing* will disgust you. You'll be able to eat a hearty meal while your child spits out her food, plays with it, and puts it back in her mouth—all right in front of you. A nice side effect of raising a baby is that your queasy stomach will be hardened and tempered by experience.

Soon enough, you'll be alone with your baby and charged with the responsibility of feeding her. It's always good to have a plan, because a hungry child is a cranky child. Learn the basics, keep a supply of food on hand, and relations with your kid will be good. Soon you will become a *baby chef,* just like me.

STEP ONE: THE ALL-LIQUID DIET

f or the first few months of your child's life, you won't need to worry much about what the kid eats. Whether she's on breast milk or formula, she will be satisfied with her liquid fare and will grow and be healthy. At some point around four months onward, though, you'll start to sense that the milk isn't hitting the spots it used to reach. The baby seems dissatisfied, irritable. She's hungry, and the bottle or breast that used to be her entire world isn't doing it for her anymore.

Then it's time for baby chef to step in.

HOW CAN YOU TOLERATE THIS FORMULAIC PABLUM?

t he time for introducing "solid" foods varies from baby to baby, and from culture to culture. A general rule of thumb is that if the baby still seems hungry after consuming milk, she probably needs something more to eat. The skilled baby chef will recognize this moment and act accordingly. Your baby will still consume her regular amount of milk or formula, and in these early days solid food is a sort of learn-to-eat bonus.

The typical first food for a baby is cereal—not Wheaties or Frankenberry, but a sort of thin gruel that you'll find in the baby section of the supermarket. It's not like any cereal that you've ever had, or will ever want to have, but babies like it. It's the first food they've ever eaten, and they don't know any better. Their stomachs and intestines have to get used to processing something besides milk, and thin cereal is about the mildest thing imaginable.

These cereals come in a few varieties: rice, barley, oats, and mixtures of grains. Mix it up with formula or breast milk. Either warm the milk in a pan or mix it up and microwave it for ten or fifteen seconds.

A lot of baby books tell you not to use microwaves to warm your child's food—the idea is that they warm unevenly, and you can end up burning your kid's palate. Think of the way you feel after taking an imprudent bite of piping-hot cheese pizza; this is definitely an experience you would prefer your child avoided. Babies prefer warm edibles, though, and the microwave is a convenient and quick means of heating up food. You can get around this problem by purchasing a colored spoon that turns white whenever the substance it comes into contact with is too hot for the baby to handle. Stir up the food well to even out the temperature. You can find heat-sensitive spoons in the baby section of the supermarket or department store. This ingenious invention will serve you well.

Once you're satisfied that you're not going to burn the baby's mouth, sit her in a comfortable place and try to give her a spoonful of warm mush. Depending on how hungry she is, she might try it. Have a camera handy, because her expression of confusion when she tastes this stuff is going to be pretty priceless. She'll probably let it all run out of her mouth, because she doesn't know how to eat yet. Marvel over how much she has yet to learn, then give her another spoonful. She'll get the idea eventually.

Let her eat as much as she wants. You'll get an idea how much she will tend to consume at each seating—typically a small, half-full teacup will be enough at first. If your child is only a few months old, she really doesn't *need* the cereal to survive, not if she's drinking enough milk. The cereal is a supplement to her diet at this point.

STEP TWO: "DAD, ENOUGH GRUEL. WHAT ELSE DO YOU HAVE?"

E ventually she's going to get sick of rice cereal. Who can blame her? If you're one of those saints who eats a bowl of oatmeal every morning, then more power to you. The rest of us tire of that stuff pretty quickly, and babies are no different.

It's time to move on to the world of baby food. Fortunately, most baby food that comes in jars is labeled by age—so you don't have to worry too much about serving something wildly inappropriate. Just remember that the baby can't chew anything yet, and her food has to be mashed into a pastelike consistency.

This is when things start to get fun. By now your child is used to being spoon-fed, and her motor skills aren't advanced enough yet for her to demand the spoon so she can hurl gobs of fruit paste onto the front of your wool sweater. Like a little baby bird, she'll look up at you with her maw wide open. You can watch her taste each flavor for the first time. And, for a while at least, you probably won't have any trouble getting her to eat her vegetables.

Take note of what foods she likes and dislikes. It's generally a good idea to try to balance fruits and vegetables, but don't get too stressed out when she doesn't eat her bananas during her ten A.M. meal. As long as a baby is drinking formula or breast milk, she's already getting balanced nutrition.

It's also important that mealtimes be enjoyable for the baby; they are a time of discovery and pleasure. If you're stressed out about what she's eating, and how much of it, she's going to pick up on that. The last thing you want is for mealtime to become a time of stress, demands, and expectations. If you let her, she'll develop her own relationship to food and feeding, one that will be easygoing and geared toward satisfying her needs rather than yours.

There's a pretty big variety of baby food out there. Small babies tend to like bananas, pears, apples, berries diluted with other fruits, sweet potatoes, carrots, peas. Oranges are too acidic for right now. You can also buy organic baby food at the health-food store and at some supermarkets, if you're concerned about pesticides and additives.

A note: There's a school of thought that says you should only introduce a new food to your baby once every week. This way, if your baby has an allergic reaction, it will be easy for you to identify the culprit. The general notion is that it's good to keep things easy and gradual for babies. I agree, although I didn't strictly adhere to the once-a-week rule. Sometimes I cut the time between new foods down to three or four days. In Natasha's case, she was hearty and didn't seem to be allergic to anything. In fact, she didn't even seem to *dislike* any kind of food. Each child is different. Tailor the time period between introducing new foods to how well your child responds to change.

Another option is to make your own baby food. It's a lot cheaper, although it's a bit of a hassle. You can buy a food mill at a cooking or baby store. This will enable you to mill a couple of bananas at one time and store extra supplies in the refrigerator. It's pretty easy to do, but if you're pressed for time you might want to cut corners and buy the stuff premade.

I really enjoyed the baby-food phase. Natasha always liked to eat, and baby food is extremely easy to prepare and serve. The process is inevitably messy, though, so invest in a couple of plastic bibs. If you're feeling hungry, have a spoonful or two yourself. It's not half bad, and your kid will probably be extremely pleased to see you sharing her meal.

Baby Chef Secret #1:

Once your child starts on baby food, she might decide that the cereal she used to love is now for squares. She'll let out a squawk of protest as soon as she sees it coming. *Dad, what are you trying to do to me? That is so yesterday.*

First of all, get used to this feeling. It certainly will not be the first time your child changes her likes and dislikes on a dime, making you feel like you're hopelessly behind the times. Wait until she's thirteen and you try to buy her a CD—or whatever we'll be listening to then. *Dad, I don't listen to the Smiley Happy Elves anymore. No one does. Now we like the Screaming Bloody Murderers.*

But you still have a big box of cereal on the shelf, and you don't feel like throwing it out. Anyway, the cereal is fortified with all kinds of nutrition, and you want her to eat at least a few spoonfuls in the morning. Try making a mixture of a favorite fruit baby food—bananas, typically—and the remaining cereal. The resulting flavorful mush is much more likely to be met with a hungry grunt and open mouth. Remember to heat it up. Would *you* want cold oatmeal in the morning?

Baby Chef Secret #2:

Sometimes you will meet with resistance when you feed your child. She simply might not be hungry: she might be in a bad mood. If it becomes a pattern, it might be because she's sick of what you're feeding her. Try mixing up the menu. What the hell, see if she likes bananas and pears mushed up together. If nothing else, the novelty might work, at least once.

Another option is to throw in a dash of salt with her vegetables, or a dash of fruit juice with her baby food, for added flavor. Some people have problems with the idea of their child eating *any* salt or sugar—and fruit juice really is a form of sugar. If you're worried about this, don't do it. But if you feel like your child isn't eating enough, or that she doesn't like her food, give it a shot. Babies develop habits like anyone else, and next time you might leave out the salt and see that she's into a new routine of eating heartily. I hope so, anyway.

Remember, babies tend to like their food served warm. They're like us. If someone gave me a plate of cold peas I would politely send it back to the kitchen. Or else throw it on the floor and burst into tears, depending on my mood.

STEP THREE: THINGS YOU WOULD RECOGNIZE AS FOOD

A fter a while you'll find it's time to stretch the parameters of what you feed your baby. This is when things start to get really fun. As with mushed-up food, you want to let a little time pass between new foods. But now you're working toward a great goal, the Holy Grail of baby feeding: the moment when the baby, more or less, is eating the same thing you're eating.

An unavoidable aspect of the child's first year is teething. Teething makes children irritable, makes them drool, and can make you miserable. If you think your child is experiencing inordinate amounts of teething pain, consider using an over-the-counter analgesic liquid—it comes in low-dose baby varieties.

The good side of teething is that, when it's over (but don't kid yourself—sometimes it seems like there's *always* a new tooth coming in), your child will have a new tooth. This means she'll soon be able to eat a greater variety of foods. Buy her a baby toothbrush—they come in an antichoking ring shape—and start to teach her to brush. You can buy baby toothpaste, which they all seem to like the taste of. Soon she'll want to do it herself. She might not be terribly efficient at it, but you'll be glad later that she learned how.

Once a child is older than six months, her stomach is basically able to digest the same foods as ours. But use common sense. Really spicy foods can cause a problem, not to mention foods that are heavily acidic, like tomatoes. When you take your child to the pediatrician for a checkup, remember to ask any questions about feeding you might have. For instance, *Is it all right if I give my daughter five-alarm chili? I noticed her eyes watering the last time I did, and the gas was almost unbearable. For me.*

In other words, don't push it too much at first. Babies like things quiet and mild, but you can gradually get them used to the raucous world of macaroni and cheese and refried beans.

Keep in mind as well that your kid doesn't have many teeth. Her food has to be served in small pieces, and you don't want to give her anything that requires a lot of chewing. The fact is, the ten-month-old child is probably gulping and swallowing most of her food without even bothering to gum it. But you'll find out all about it when you change her diaper the next morning.

Baby Chef Secret #3

Some fruits, like apples and pears, will be a little hard for a baby to eat. But they love the flavor. Cut up an apple or under-ripe pear into little cubes, then toss them into a glass or plastic container. Pour enough water into the container to cover the fruit and nuke the whole thing for about twenty to thirty seconds. The fruit will come out soft enough for the baby to deal with. It will also be as hot as molten lava. Try running cold water over the fruit until it cools all the way through. Stir, then run more cool water over it. Taste a couple of samples to make sure they aren't too hot on the inside. Serve with pride.

As your baby attains a greater level of motor skill, she's going to want to get more involved with her meals. In fact, she's going to *demand* it. *Encourage* this impulse. Buy a high chair, put the food in front of her, and let her feed herself as well as she can before intervening. Before long, your partner, you, and your child will be able to actually sit down and eat a meal together in relative peace. Now *that's* living.

Baby Chef Secret #4:

Babies love pasta. Mac 'n' cheese, spaghetti, rigatoni. Serve with butter, sauce, a little melted mozzarella. Make sure you reduce the pasta to baby-bite-size pieces. And always overcook it, the softer the better.

Baby Chef Secret #5:

Your child is going to figure out that bananas taste better than peas. Go figure. For the moment, however, you are still smarter than your child. Heat up a little dollop of frozen peas or corn and find a creative place to slip the veggies into your daughter's food. She'll probably be onto you before long, but by then you will have devised another devilish stratagem.

CHEZ BABY—SPECIALTIES DU JOUR

H ere are some suggestions for baby meals. Mix and match various foods as you see fit, and as your baby responds. You'll know from daily experience what foods your child likes and is ready to eat.

For all meals, adjust portion size to suit your baby's needs. Let your child eat as much as she wants, without pressuring her to eat more. When you're cooking or preparing food for your child, it's good to make more than you think she's going to want. You never know when she's going to go through a growth spurt and eat you under the table. Portion sizes are suggested with this in mind, and are approximate. You can eat the leftovers and cement your reputation as the family's human garbage disposal.

Notice that each of these meals requires very little actual cooking. No matter how hopeless you might be in the kitchen, you're more than capable of whipping up a tasty meal that your kid will enjoy.

Again, *don't sweat it*. A couple of times I've gotten ambitious and made elaborate lunches for Natasha. One was pan-fried tofu with soy sauce; the other was a cheese quesadilla with refried beans. Both reduced her to tears and made her extremely pissed off with me. She just wasn't ready. *Too bad.* That left more for me.

Meal #1: Old Sturdy Breakfast—Serve Anytime

   1 frozen waffle, cooked in toaster and ripped into
      little pieces (from here on, we'll assume that you're
      reducing all the food into appropriate pieces)
   1 egg, fried in light butter
  ½ banana

Natasha and I ate this one two or three times a week for months. It was great, because I made enough for both of us and we were able to enjoy a slow leisurely meal together.

Meal #2: Tofu Surprise

  ½ cup soft tofu, cubed
  ½ pear, softened and cubed (see above)
   1 baby arrowroot cookie

Tofu is a good source of protein, and a lot of babies are willing to eat it raw until they realize that it has no flavor. Arrowroot cookies can be found in the baby section at the supermarket. Babies like them. It's a cookie and not really nutritious, though, so wait until the end of the meal to offer it.

Meal #3: Fromage du Jour

  ½ cup mild cheese (jack, mozzarella, soft cheddar),
      cubed

½ apple, softened and cubed (see above)
3–4 saltine crackers, broken

Babies love cheese. This meal is a big favorite with Natasha, who enjoys a cheese-and-cracker assortment as much as the rest of us. Omit the usual red wine.

Meal #4: L'Essence du Mac

½ cup macaroni and cheese
¼ cup steamed cauliflower
½ kiwi fruit

Macaroni and cheese is pretty close to being the ultimate kid food. I make a box, give Natasha as much as she wants, and eat the rest myself. She also enjoys steamed broccoli and cauliflower, but be sure to oversteam the vegetables so they're extremely soft. As for the kiwi, be careful not to give your kid too much. More acidic fruits can cause an upset stomach and diarrhea and lead to diaper rash.

Meal #5: Some of Daddy's Food

1 beans-and-rice burrito from a take-out place
½ cup applesauce
2 graham crackers

You don't always have to make a meal just for your child. Buy yourself a burrito for lunch and remove some rice and beans for your baby's main course. She'll enjoy picking them up. Go easy on the salsa, though—serve your child's food without it, putting it on yours separately. Serve the graham crackers last, as a dessert.

Meal #6: Leftover Surprise

  2 baby meat sticks
  ½ cup egg noodles, specially prepared or leftovers
  ¼ cup sliced steamed carrots

When and if you decide to introduce meat into your baby's diet, you can buy meat sticks in the baby section of the supermarket. These are essentially little Vienna sausages that are extra soft and suitable for a baby to feed herself. This meal is a leftover surprise since you made egg noodles or some other pasta the night before and, because you're so smart, saved some for heating up the next day for your baby's lunch. Put in a teaspoon of water if you microwave, so the noodles don't get too dry.

Baby Chef Secret #6:

For small children, the *experience* of a meal can be just as important as the taste of the food. If your child isn't eating as much as you'd like, try to make the experience fun. Sit close to her and talk to her through the meal. Play some of her favorite music in the background. Pretty soon she'll want to take over. Give her her food in small cups or plastic dishes, give her a baby spoon, and let her go to town. She'll be ineffectual at first, but you can hand-feed her some morsels while she's messing around and having a good time. As long as your baby enjoys mealtime, you're ahead of the game.

Meal #7: Lunch in Under One Minute

  ½ flour or corn tortilla, steamed in a damp paper
      towel in the microwave for 30 seconds
  ½ cup whole yogurt, fruit or plain
  ¼ cup cubed peach

You can get this one together quickly if you're running late for mealtime and your daughter is getting crabby from hunger. Yogurt is one of the great baby foods—it's easy to eat and extremely good for kids. Start a small baby out on plain unflavored yogurt and move on to more exotic varieties. Buy whole yogurt—not the low-fat or nonfat kind—babies need the extra fat to grow, and they're a long way from having to worry about fat and cholesterol in their diet.

Meal #8: I Forgot to Shop

  1 slice white bread
  1 cup frozen peas, boiled, steamed, or microwaved
 ½ cup cottage cheese

Babies are so forgiving. You can whip up an easy meal like this one, emptying out the dregs of the fridge, and your child might enjoy it as much as one you put a lot more effort into. Remember to try to vary the texture, color, and consistency of the various foods you serve at each meal. For a small child, eating is as much about sensory discovery as it is about satisfying hunger.

Baby Chef Secret #7

    Take a good look at the baby section of the supermarket and see what your options are. It's a good idea to stockpile a few items in case you don't have time to cook anything, or in case the food you're having for dinner is unsuitable for a small child. You can buy fruit presliced—although it's a lot cheaper to slice your own, and requires relatively little effort, sometimes a prepackaged fruit cup saves the day. There are usually a few varieties of cookies and biscuits available that are made extra soft for toothless babies. These are good to have on hand for dessert.

Baby Chef Secret #8

Juice is baby soda pop. They love it because it's so sweet. Why shouldn't they? A cup of apple juice might be the sweetest thing your kid has ever tasted in her life.

There are drawbacks, however. Juice contains sugar. It's naturally occurring sugar, but sugar nonetheless. Which is why you need to seriously consider restricting how much juice your kid drinks. Maybe you like to quaff a half-dozen Mountain Dews every day, but do you want your nine-month-old to do the same?

When you serve juice, either in a baby bottle or a sipping cup, dilute it with water. I usually do a mixture of one-third juice to two-thirds water. Babies also enjoy drinking plain water—remember, they're people, too. Offer a cup of water to your son when he gets up from a nap and is overheated and dehydrated. Have one yourself.

This should get you squared away for the first year of feeding your baby. As you can see, it's a pretty elastic process. Be sure to talk to your pediatrician about foods to avoid, but outside of those restrictions you can feed your baby whatever she can handle. Remember to have fun. Shared mealtimes should be enjoyable bonding experiences for both of you. And when your kid holds out a half-chewed piece of cheese daubed in strawberry yogurt, be a good sport and accept it. Just don't think about where it's been.

Later Days

Big Baby Stuff: Sleeping, Accidents, Handling Advice, and Baby Moods

A child's graduation from newborn infancy into hearty babyhood is a fantastic thing to watch. Pretty soon you realize that, in a couple of months, your son is going to be a year old.

OK, let's all say it together: *They grow up so fast.*

You feel immeasurable pride with each step forward in your child's progress: holding his head upright, then sitting and crawling, then the tentative first steps. He learns to eat finger food on his own, and he learns his first couple of words, *Dada* hopefully among them.

There's another side to the coin, of course—the frustration, the deadening fatigue, the sense of being overwhelmed that each parent feels at some point. But probably by now you've learned that the situation is ever-changing, and that things will always get better. Then maybe worse again for a little while. Then better again.

This is the nature of fatherhood.

HELPING EACH OTHER OUT

W hen Natasha was about seven months old, my mother got sick and I had to rush back to Ohio to visit her. Mom required surgery, and I stayed until she was in recovery; then I had to get back to Minnesota to resume taking care of Natasha.

It was a hard time, and knowing how much Natasha needed me made it, in a sense, more difficult. It also made it better and easier for me to deal with, because I could draw upon the bond between my child and me for strength. As long as I was helping her to be happy, I was doing something good with my life. Things could happen that were beyond my control, but I knew that if I worked hard I could have a positive effect on the world.

Having a child deepens your sense of life. You begin to realize how profound the bonds are between yourself and the few other people that we call close family and friends. You're getting older yourself, and sometimes it's easy to focus on how much you have to lose, how precarious all of our lives really are.

It's called growing up, I suppose. It isn't easy. It can reduce a grown man to tears sometimes. Pick up your child, hold him, tell him you love him. Give your partner a kiss. This is life, and it's a beautiful thing.

WHICH IS ALL WELL AND GOOD, BUT . . .

. . . my kid won't go to sleep at night.

It's hard to ponder the deeper dimensions of existence when you haven't slept eight hours straight in almost a year. Your child wakes up at two in the morning and demands to be consoled. You explain to him, *You know, I don't get to nap all day.*

But it doesn't do any good. He doesn't like to nap in the crib, he doesn't like to be put to bed at night. He's all over the place. And so are you. Something has to be done.

The fact is that most young babies get up at around six in the morning. This is bad enough, but to compound the problem they often wake a couple of times during the night. For months Natasha followed a pretty predictable pattern: go to bed around seven, then wake at approximately ten, one, and three. At six she was up for good.

I thought I was going to lose my mind.

Today Sarah reminds me that I am not exactly in a perfect position to complain. "About ninety-five percent of the time, I was the one getting up to deal with her," she says. "You complain, but you weren't even the one bearing the brunt."

Guilty as charged. But I did wake up each time, if only to grumble and roll over, and it exhausted me. What can I say? I'm pretty good when I'm awake, I'm useless when I'm half asleep.

You should get up and deal with the child when he wakes. Don't be like me. Be *better* than me.

That being said, there are a couple of schools of thought regarding getting your kid to sleep through the night. The most popular one, which you'll hear about all the time, is called *Ferberizing*. The theory is that kids need to learn to sleep on their own, in the crib—not by associating sleep with a nipple or being rocked.

Here's the deal: put your baby in his crib, say good night, and leave the room. He will probably begin to cry. Wait five minutes, go in, comfort him without picking him up, then leave. Wait ten minutes before going in again, then fifteen, until he falls asleep. Reassure the baby in a gentle tone, but don't pick him up and don't give him the things he associates with his previous sleep rituals.

We tried this with Natasha, and it didn't really work. Then again, we weren't the sort of consistent taskmasters this method requires. If we have another child, I think I'm going to be more hard-hearted.

Some babies don't respond well to this technique, and some

parents don't deal well with listening to their child's desperate cries for what can turn into long periods of time. I have always suspected that some parents try this method on kids who are too young to deal with it. Babies have to be at least about four months old before this technique can be attempted on them. But who can say? If it works, and the child learns to sleep through the night in his crib, then everyone is probably better off. Just keep in mind that you're dealing with a baby, and that you need to cut him some slack.

Of course, this mentality led to Natasha's not sleeping through the night until she was ten months old. I consider us lucky. It takes some kids even longer.

Sometimes the issue of sleeping through the night is almost a competitive thing among parents. Without really thinking about what they're doing—let's give them the benefit of the doubt—they fall into the trap of comparing. *Oh, your little Amadeus isn't sleeping through the night yet. How terrible for you. My little Madeleine has been sleeping through the night since she was in the womb.*

My experience was that Natasha took each step in her developmental progress when she was *ready*. This included sitting up, crawling, sleeping through the night, weaning herself from the breast, and walking. I tried not to measure her progress against that of the other babies I knew, because the development of each baby is different. I didn't want to put any pressure on her to take difficult steps in her life. There'll be plenty of *that* later on, from a rich variety of sources.

Natasha had problems going to sleep. It's just one of those things. Nap time has always been a little difficult, and she didn't sleep through the night until she was ten months old and my wife and I were almost at the end of our rope. I've always thought it was because she was so hyperaware, so engaged with

the world. I think she has trouble letting go of consciousness because there's so much going on in her mind.

There have been periods when she would be put in her crib
at seven or eight to go to bed for the night. She would be exhausted—rubbing her eyes, yawning, breaking into tears of frustration. But then, after half an hour of silence on the baby
monitor, she would start to sob. Then wail. And then would
come the pterodactyl, the throaty cry that means there's no going back, for anyone.

Sarah and I would look at each other. Whose turn was it to
go upstairs and deal with her? We were both frustrated, knowing
that the baby was sleepy but unwilling, or unable, to find a restful
groove.

I'd walk up the creaky stairs, trudge toward our bedroom.
The sounds of crying and wailing would grow louder and louder
until I opened the door to Natasha's little room. Then the cries
would become almost deafening. Natasha would be lying with
her eyes closed, off in a world of her own, screaming for some
kind of comfort that she probably didn't even understand she
needed.

I'd bend over the crib and pick her up. Immediately her tiny
body would conform to the shape of my chest. Her head felt
hard against my shoulder blade. Her thumb went into her mouth
as she completely relaxed against me. Her body was loose-
limbed, pliable, immediately lost in a posture of early sleep that
was totally devoid of self-consciousness. I'd think of adults, of
the stiffness that sets into our bodies as the years pass, the awk-
ward poses of rest that become necessary in adulthood. And I'd
hold my daughter close to me, talking to her softly as she fell
asleep again, thinking about how hard it was to be a baby, how
many challenges she had to face daily. And I'd feel the innocence
of her form against mine. She was a little animal, calm and secure
in her father's arms.

There's another sleeping-through-the-night technique called scheduled awakenings. Essentially you try to beat the baby to the punch by waking him about fifteen minutes before the time when he usually gets up and starts crying. If he gets up at three, go in there and get him up at two forty-five. As he learns that you're his alarm clock, start to extend his sleeping periods, with the gradual goal of having him expect you to come in and wake him in the morning.

This sounds rough to me, and I never tried it. First of all, *you* have to get yourself up to wake the child. And sometimes, I've heard, it's pretty hard to get the baby to wake up. Besides, you'll be violating the sacrosanct truism: never wake a sleeping baby.

Remember not to get obsessed by your kid's sleep patterns. No matter what your friends' kids are doing, waking during the night at six months old is *perfectly normal.* Try what works for you and your baby, but keep in mind that you may be creating anxiety that may be detrimental to your overall goals—and which, in the end, may make him enjoy his life a little bit less.

Good luck. It took Natasha ten months, and then one night she slept through until morning. Within a week it was her regular pattern: go to bed around eight, get up around seven-thirty or eight the next morning.

It took a while. But it was *heaven.*

THREE'S COMPANY; THREE'S ALSO A . . .

You come home from the hospital, exhausted, and the three of you go to bed together. You sense the tiny presence of the infant between you and your partner, and you wake slightly when he gurgles and cries in the middle of the night, demanding to be fed.

Morning comes, and your partner gets up to take a shower. She leaves the two of you together. You half wake; maybe you put your arm gently around your son or pull him close to your chest. Pretty soon you're breathing in unison. He wakes up, tries to focus on you, to become familiar with your face.

Move forward three months. The baby's still sleeping with you, and it isn't so great anymore. He kicks in the night, waking you up. He shifts and grunts. He lets out cries in his sleep. It's worse than sleeping with a neurotic cat. One morning you wake up, bleary-eyed, and realize that it's time for him to start sleeping in his crib at night.

This is how it worked for me. Natasha simply got too big, too restless, for us to sleep with her in the bed. So we moved her into the crib. It was tough for a while, and she woke up and cried a lot. We had new problems to deal with. But it was *time,* and we all seemed to know it. A new phase had begun.

As with so many other babyhood issues, there are combating orthodoxies on this issue. Listen to them and sort the issue out for yourself. And remember that there's no absolute wrong thing to do, and that your family knows what's best for itself.

In September of 1999, the Consumer Product Safety Commission (CPSC) issued a report that concluded parents should *never* sleep in the same bed with children younger than two. The report cited an average of sixty-four children a year over an eight-year period who died as a result of sleeping in bed with their parents.

This report struck me as hogwash, and a lot of fire immediately erupted on the other side of the battlements.

For my part, I had to match up those sixty-four unfortunate children against the number who died of sudden infant death syndrome (SIDS) in their cribs. It's a terrible tragedy, but it happens. Children die, often for reasons that medicine can't explain.

One useful fact came out of the study: many of the children who died in their parents' bed did so as a result of becoming trapped between the mattress and the headboard and then suffocating or being strangled by bedding. A suggestion was offered: a "co-sleeper" bassinet, which attaches to the bed but affords the baby its own protected sleeping area. This might be a practical solution for you if this study causes you concern.

On the other side of the argument are parents who believe in the *family bed,* or *attachment parenting.* These terms pretty much explain themselves, and neither interested me much. Parenthood was hard enough without getting attached to some sort of dogma. Then again, maybe that's what attracts some parents: a set of rules to follow, a philosophy to espouse. Whatever floats your boat.

Natasha slept between us until she got annoying, and then we all made a change. Many pediatricians feel that sleeping with newborns is useful for their development, but all I know is that it *felt* good. It also made the numerous nighttime feedings (every couple of hours) much easier for Sarah.

I worried about crushing Natasha—the first night. Then I realized that I was aware of her in my sleep, that I was keeping to my side of the bed, and that the three of us were sleeping together like humans have since we existed on the earth.

Don't let anyone tell you what to do. Each side will present the issue as a pressing moral concern, and try to make you feel like a bad father if you don't do what they say. Well, people are always trying to make you feel like a bad person for not following their party line. It happens throughout life. Why should fatherhood be any different?

Do what makes you and your family happy. If you're worried, take action. If you're not, enjoy the intimacy. I can still remember the sound of Natasha's soft breathing next to me in bed, the heat coming from her tiny body.

I also remember the relief I felt when she moved out. *Finally,* a little room to stretch. I imagined Natasha in her crib, sucking her thumb, thinking the same thing: *Finally, some room to sleep without the giants. I wondered if they'd ever get the hint. I mean, I kept kicking them and waking them up. Some people never get the message.*

Let's say you've finally gotten your baby to start sleeping through the night. You proudly note that it's been almost two weeks straight that he's gone to bed at around seven or eight, then slept quietly and peacefully until six or seven the next morning. You start getting some sleep, the bags under your eyes start to go away. It's bliss.

Then one night, around nine or so, he starts crying. You glance at the monitor nervously. His cries get louder and louder, until finally something has to be done. You're able to console him and get him to return to bed, then at midnight he's up again and you have to start the entire process over again. Your precarious edifice of peace is shot, and you feel like you're back to square one.

Well, it's actually *not* as bad as that. Once your child has learned to regulate himself and sleep in his crib, he's gained a skill that isn't going to go away entirely. But there will be setbacks at various developmental stages, and he's going to have rough nights out of the blue—usually just when you thought you had everything under control.

Some pediatricians tie these sleep disruptions to developmental breakthroughs, and from living with Natasha I think they're right. She had been sleeping better than she ever had until, one summer night, she learned how to manipulate the refrigerator magnets. She played with them in rapt fascination and focus until bedtime and then, about an hour later, was awake in her crib crying. Babies are like us. When they have a lot on their minds, they have a rough time sleeping. Eventually, though, they get back on track. If it feels like two steps forward and one step back, that's because it is.

BABY STUNTMEN: DUST 'EM OFF AND GET 'EM BACK IN THE GAME

First they start inching across the floor. Then they crawl, millimeter by tenuous millimeter. Pretty soon they can pull themselves up and stand next to a table. Something happens in a flash, and your precious son is bleeding from the forehead. You freak out, he freaks out, and in an instant the whole family is in a state of shock.

What just happened?

When your child becomes more mobile, he also exponentially increases his capacity for inflicting harm on himself. Get used to it. Kids are clumsy. Remember when you were a child, when you always had bruises on your arms and skinned knees? I think I probably get about a bruise a year now, although I *did* almost saw off my thumb trying to shorten the Christmas tree last year.

I've seen a lot of things I wish I hadn't. Natasha has teetered over backward and smacked her head on the floor more times than I care to remember. One time she pitched forward, cracked her mouth on the edge of a table, and started bleeding from her gums. I saw her try to catch herself from falling and lurch into an unfortunate impromptu cartwheel. Another time she pushed down on the edge of a metal pail and sent its opposite side smacking into her face, like the Skipper stepping on a bamboo rake on *Gilligan's Island*. Once I saw her hurt herself three times in the space of a single minute; she was tired, and everything she touched turned into a bludgeon that she somehow turned on herself.

It's hard to watch, but it happens—to every child. With each leap forward, your child is going to have to confront his limitations. He'll get frustrated, angry, humiliated. He'll reach out for comfort, then push your hands away. He'll get pissed off.

Sometimes Natasha looks like a combatant in an Ali-Frazier fight. Scrapes on the forehead, a cut around the eye, a bruise on her chin—all self-inflicted. It hurts to see her like this, but I know that there's no way I can protect her from physics and gravity. *Fall down, go boom.*

The good news is that small children are more flexible than us, and their bones are far less brittle. And, from what I've seen, their skin heals much faster than ours.

There are a lot of products available for "baby-proofing" your house, and you have to decide which ones will work for you. You should cover unused electrical outlets, and make sure poisons are out of reach or inside cabinets that a small child can't open. Beyond the obvious dangers, there are table edges, stairs, an entire *universe* of ways that your kid can eventually hurt himself.

Remember that you can't protect him from everything. Falling down is a normal part of learning to move. Babies are amazingly resilient. The rule of thumb on head injuries is that if the baby is crying, he's probably going to be fine as soon as the shock and humiliation wear off. It's when the baby doesn't react that you have to worry about head injury. Keep an eye on your kid and be there to dust him off when he falls. And marvel at his sturdiness—imagine taking a fall like that and being able to play with blocks again five minutes later. Natasha takes tumbles on a regular basis that would land me in the hospital.

MY ADVICE IS TO STOP
GIVING ME ADVICE

Be prepared for all the advice you're going to receive. From your family and friends. From strangers. *Especially* from strangers.

You might be tempted to ask *What's the problem? Do you*

think I'm an idiot who has no idea what he's doing with this baby?

Don't ask. Because that's precisely what they're thinking about you. Don't make them say it.

I took Natasha out on a winter day to the market. She was wearing a snowsuit, three layers of warm clothes, a big hat. If anything, she was uncomfortable because she was too hot.

I looked up from my deep perusal of the pastry rack to see a woman staring at me. The baby was in my arms, lost in the abstract world of the newborn.

I looked away from the woman, then back again. No doubt about it, she was staring at me.

"You shouldn't take that baby out on a day like this," she said. "It's too cold. She should be inside."

Well, thank you very much.

In the springtime I took Natasha to the market again. We go to the market all the time. We have to go someplace, after all; might as well get something to eat.

There was a sample display of sausage. An older woman was frying up links on a little hot plate, serving them skewered by toothpicks on little paper doilies. I wondered how many I could eat before she made me go away.

She looked up from the hot plate. "Where are her *stah-kins?*" she asked in a tobacco rasp.

"Beg your pardon?"

"Her *stah-kins!* It's too cold!"

Oh, her stockings. The baby wasn't wearing any shoes or socks. It was also about seventy degrees outside.

"She's fine," I said. "How about some of that sausage?"

"It's too cold out," she insisted. "She needs to be wearing *stah-kins!*"

Well, thank you very much.

Another variation on this theme is that people will admire your baby, then start to criticize it.

"Oh she's so *beautiful,*" they'll gush.

"Well, thanks," you'll say. "*I* certainly think so."

"But she's too *small*. Isn't she getting enough to eat?"

"She eats fine. At least two or three times a week."

"What's that mark on her head? Has a doctor looked at it?"

"Yes, and it's a rare skin condition. Very contagious. Would you like to touch it?"

"She's so calm. Almost too calm, do you know what I mean? Is she always like this?"

"Yes, because she is very unintelligent."

"Is she warm enough in that jacket?"

"She'd better be, because we live in a sewer drain."

Another variant of this is the question you will be asked by strangers many times: *Is she sleeping through the night yet?*

"Yes, she is. And she's also almost mastered calculus. Any other questions?"

"Yes. Why is she so pale? Is she eating enough?"

Thank you very much.

SAILING THE STORMY SEAS OF BABY MOODS

here's a wonderful period at around eight or nine months, and lasting until the baby is about a year old, when all is great with the world. Enjoy it. Things are going to start to change as your baby gradually becomes a toddler—and for the worse, although it won't be as bad as some sources will lead you to believe.

The baby's emotional range starts to grow, and with it come dark clouds of negativity, temper, defiance, and mania.

There's no other way to describe it.

At various points in their development, babies experience what is called *separation anxiety*. In short, this means that they get upset and cry when a parent or loved one leaves the room. This is because they're picking up on a concept called *object permanence,* which means that they understand that when you leave you're actually gone. You *could* be there, but you're not, and it freaks them out. Up until that point, it's pretty much been "out of sight, out of mind."

Separation anxiety takes many forms, and you need to realize that they're all very normal—in fact, even though it can be upsetting or inconvenient, you can take solace in knowing that your baby is going through a real breakthrough in his mental development.

One form of separation anxiety involves the shedding of tears whenever Mom or Dad leaves, or even strays too far away. Fortunately most babies can be distracted, and even more fortunately, they soon learn that you're coming back eventually. You can tell that your baby has this anxiety when the moment he picks up that things are changing—let's say, when you put on your coat—he latches on to you with a baby-monkey death grip. Gently peel the baby from your chest and hand him over to the sitter. If he's really upset, get out quick. He'll be all right soon.

This stage is often accompanied by a real restlessness of the spirit, along with *stranger anxiety.* Babies become less trusting of strangers, sometimes less friendly in general. They are starting to understand that the world is not completely composed of family members and trusted settings. The sight of a stranger smiling can even make the infant burst into tears. Reassure the baby, then reassure the stranger by saying "It's not you. It's just a stage."

Which it is—one of many to come.

The good news: it sets in gradually, and the months just before a baby's first birthday are a sort of golden age. Natasha was invariably happy, her sly and wry sense of humor flowered, and she was inordinately proud of each new step in her development. My heart swelled with love for her, more than ever.

One night she finally said it. *Dada.* Natasha looked at me and said Dada. I could have floated off into the sky.

The excitement of communication when your child first starts to vocalize is immense. It's an amazing thing when the grunts and groans of an infant start to transform into sounds; pretty soon, you'll hear for the first time what your baby's voice sounds like. It's a sound you won't be able to get enough of.

One night Sarah and I were sitting in bed with Natasha and the cats. Natasha loves the cats so much that the awesome sight of their furry coats still makes her avert her eyes sometimes, like a believer looking away from the face of some mythic deity. Natasha was staring at Nora, laughing, occasionally daring to reach out and touch her fur. Nora was purring softly, secure in the knowledge that if she didn't rake the baby with her claws she would eventually get an MSG-soaked treat.

"You love Nora, don't you?" Sarah asked her. Natasha squealed with delight.

"Can you say 'Nora'?" I said. Natasha looked up at me, faint comprehension playing over her features.

"Nora," Sarah said. "Nor-a. Nor-a."

I joined in, pointing at the cat. *Nor-a. Nor-a.* The cat looked around nervously. *It's finally happened,* Nora was thinking. *They've gone completely insane. I wonder if I should try to run for it.*

"Nor-a. Nor-a," Sarah and I said in unison.

Natasha opened her mouth. She pointed at Nora. Sarah and I went silent with expectation. Was it really about to happen?

"Laba," Natasha said, pointing at Nora. Her voice was crystal clear, those two syllables pronounced with complete certainty.

Laba. Ah, the joys of communication. What the hell? we thought. We called Nora *Laba* for about a week. Natasha seemed pleased.

A one-year-old baby is a magnificent creature. He's coming into his own, developing intellectually, emotionally, and physically, at a rate that is almost hard to believe. There were times when I looked at Natasha and asked myself, *Is this really my little girl? She wasn't anything like this two weeks ago.*

Enjoy it. You earned it. Your baby calls you by name. He brings you things to look at. He loves you.

And all of the trials and effort, all of the hard times and the sense of desperation, seem kind of far away and hazy now. It wasn't really that bad at first, was it?

Oh, but it was. You're beginning to indulge in *selective memory.* Well, join the club. After all, who could possibly focus on the negative in the presence of such a delightful, energetic, curious, and happy child?

No one. But try to remember a little of the bad times. Because some guy is going to come up to you and ask, *What's it like?*

Remember to tell him that there's a lot of good and a lot of bad. That there will be times when he will feel as though he can't take it anymore, as well as times when he is the happiest man on the planet.

And remember to tell him that it's all worth it.

Happy Birthday, Little Girl

For Natasha's first birthday we decided to throw a party—as much for us as for her. It was an excuse to see some friends on a Sunday afternoon, another attempt to stay connected with our social life and not fall into a black hole of insular family isolation.

Brynnar brought Natasha a warm winter hat. Teddie and Chris brought a beautiful red sweater. Baby Henry came, along with his parents, Gary and Julie. Our friends Dave and Lisa arrived, unaware that in a couple of months they were going to conceive a baby. It was a good feeling to know that we still had friends, people we cared about and who still wanted to hang out with us even though our lives had changed so much in the past year.

As for Natasha, the *czarina* turned shy. With so many people around, she wanted to be held by me or Sarah the entire time. She sucked her thumb and looked contemplative. She had a stomach flu, so there was to be no traditional cake-smearing in front of the cameras. We knew her well, and she was saying to us without words: *Please, I'm delicate. Just hold me.*

I moved from the living room to the kitchen, Natasha's

twenty-pound body against mine. I rocked her, talked to people, poured myself a glass of wine. Every so often Natasha would look up at me with her lovely brown eyes, just soaking me in, checking to make sure she was safe and secure.

"One year," I whispered to her. "Can you believe it?"

She looked up again, a little inquisitive. A flash of playfulness crossed the corners of her mouth around the thumb she was sucking.

"It's been a good year, baby," I said low, into her ear.

Nothing was ever going to be the same again. Of course, I remembered my life before Natasha, but now I could no longer imagine a world in which she didn't exist. She had grown from a zygote to a little person who called me Daddy—all in the space of less than two years.

It wasn't easy. But then, nothing worth having ever is.

I knew that I had turned the corner from maintaining a helpless infant to becoming a real father. Soon I would have to discipline Natasha, talk to her, walk with her, be more than a diaper changer. The prospect was daunting, but I reminded myself how far I had come.

When I hold Natasha in my arms, singing softly to her and trying to calm her spirit, I think of all that's passed and all that's to come. I imagine my mother holding me the same way, wondering what *my* future might hold.

I think about Natasha in school. I think about her heart being broken in love. I imagine her laughing with her friends. I think about her someday being far away from me. The thought moves me to tears.

I only hope that she will be safe and happy. I hope she lives a good life, and that I can help her somehow. I hope she finds someone who loves her for who she is, and helps her become who she wants to be. I hope she always has friends. I hope she finds a place that's warm and full of light that she can call home. I want her to call me all the time. And I hope she always remembers how much her father loves her.

 INDEX

About the Author

Quinton Skinner was born and raised in Ohio, and graduated from the University of California at Santa Cruz. He has worked in the book business as a writer and editor. He is the co-author of *VH1 Behind the Music: The Day the Music Died* and the author of the upcoming *VH1 Behind the Music: Casualties of Rock*. He lives in Minneapolis with his wife and children. Since writing this book, his family has added a son, Gabriel.

© SARAH WALTER

Natasha, now two and a half years old, trained
Quinton Skinner on the ways of first-time fatherhood.
He lives with his family in Minneapolis, Minnesota.

Printed in the United States
by Baker & Taylor Publisher Services